CONTEÚDO DIGITAL PARA ALUNOS
Cadastre-se e transforme seus estudos em uma experiência única de aprendizado:

1

Entre na página de cadastro:
https://sistemas.editoradobrasil.com.br/cadastro

2

Além dos seus dados pessoais e dos dados de sua escola, adicione ao cadastro o código do aluno, que garantirá a exclusividade do seu ingresso à plataforma.

4983947A7418019

3

Depois, acesse:
https://leb.editoradobrasil.com.br/
e navegue pelos conteúdos digitais de sua coleção :D

Lembre-se de que esse código, pessoal e intransferível, é valido por um ano. Guarde-o com cuidado, pois é a única maneira de você acessar os conteúdos da plataforma.

Editora do Brasil

CB023298

MARIANA CARDIERI MENDONÇA
- Professora de inglês da rede particular de ensino
- Diplomada com *First Certificate in English*, pela Cambridge e pelo Toefl

PAULA SCHWARTZ CALDERARI
- Mestre em Ensino de Inglês pela *University of Western Ontario*
- Pós-graduada em Gestão das Organizações Educacionais pela *FAE Business School*
- Instrutora de Inglês Acadêmico na *University of Western Ontario*

APOEMA
INGLÊS
8

1ª edição
São Paulo, 2018

Dados Internacionais de Catalogação na Publicação (CIP)
(Câmara Brasileira do Livro, SP, Brasil)

Mendonça, Mariana Cardieri
    Apoema : inglês 8 / Mariana Cardieri Mendonça, Paula Schwartz Calderari. – 1. ed. – São Paulo : Editora do Brasil, 2018. – (Coleção apoema)

    ISBN 978-85-10-06954-0 (aluno)
    ISBN 978-85-10-06955-7 (professor)

    1. Inglês (Ensino fundamental) I. Calderari, Paula Schwartz. II. Título. III. Série.

18-20642   CDD-372.652

Índices para catálogo sistemático:
1. Inglês : Ensino fundamental 372.652
Maria Alice Ferreira - Bibliotecária - CRB-8/7964

1ª edição / 5ª impressão, 2024
Impresso na Forma Certa Gráfica Digital.

Avenida das Nações Unidas, 12901
Torre Oeste, 20º andar
São Paulo, SP – CEP: 04578-910
Fone: +55 11 3226-0211
www.editoradobrasil.com.br

© **Editora do Brasil S.A., 2018**
Todos os direitos reservados

Direção geral: Vicente Tortamano Avanso

Direção editorial: Felipe Ramos Poleti
Gerência editorial: Erika Caldin
Supervisão de arte e editoração: Cida Alves
Supervisão de revisão: Dora Helena Feres
Supervisão de iconografia: Léo Burgos
Supervisão de Digital: Ethel Shuña Queiroz
Supervisão de controle de processos editoriais: Marta Dias Portero
Supervisão de direitos autorais: Marilisa Bertolone Mendes

Supervisão editorial: Carla Felix Lopes
Edição: Amanda Leal e Monika Kratzer
Assistência editorial: Ana Okada e Juliana Pavoni
Auxiliar editorial: Beatriz Villanueva
Coordenação de revisão: Otacilio Palareti
Copidesque: Claudia Cantarin, Evelyn Zaidam Porting, Giselia Costa, Ridardo Liberal e Sylmara Beletti
Revisão: Alexandra Resende e Beatriz Moreira Guedes
Pesquisa iconográfica: Priscila Ferraz
Assistência de arte: Samira de Souza
Design gráfico: Anexo Produção Editorial
Capa: Megalo Design
Imagem de capa: Stockphotos/Latinstock
Ilustrações: Cristiane Viana, Christiane S. Messias, Danillo Souza, Estúdio Ornitorrinco, Ilustra Cartoon, Luiz Lentini, Marcos De Mello, Marcos Guilherme, Ronaldo Barata, Wasteresley Lima e Luiz Lentini
Coordenação de editoração eletrônica: Abdonildo José de Lima Santos
Editoração eletrônica: Adriana Tami, Armando F. Tomiyoshi, Elbert Stein, Gilvan Alves da Silva, José Anderson Campos, Sérgio Rocha, Talita Lima, Viviane Yonamine e Wlamir Miasiro
Licenciamentos de textos: Cinthya Utiyama, Jennifer Xavier, Paula Harue Tozaki e Renata Garbellini
Produção fonográfica: Jennifer Xavier e Cinthya Utiyama
Controle de processos editoriais: Bruna Alves, Carlos Nunes, Jefferson Galdino, Rafael Machado e Stephanie Paparella

HEY, STUDENT! WELCOME TO APOEMA!

A língua inglesa está cada vez mais presente nos nossos dias, seja na internet, na escola ou no trabalho. Tiramos *selfies* para postar nas redes sociais, levamos o *dog* para passear e fazemos a *homework* da escola, assistimos aos *youtubers* favoritos, vemos nossas séries e ouvimos nossas músicas em plataformas de *streaming* entre tantas outras coisas.

O conhecimento desta língua estrangeira é essencial para que possamos conhecer novos mundos, ampliar nossos horizontes e estarmos conectados com o que acontece ao nosso redor e no mundo. Por isso, é importante, e também gratificante, conhecer essa língua que conecta o mundo todo, compreender as culturas das quais ela faz parte.

Pensando nisso, nesta nova versão do **Apoema**, palavra da língua tupi que significa "aquele que vê mais longe", nosso objetivo não é apenas ensinar a língua estrangeira, mas também apresentar os diferentes lugares e culturas em que o inglês é o idioma nativo.

Nossa proposta é apresentar a língua inglesa de forma dinâmica, atual, interessante e ligada ao mundo real para que você possa usá-la para se comunicar, entendê-la e escrevê-la de forma fluente, interagindo com o mundo e expandindo seus horizontes, ou seja, vendo mais longe.

LET'S GET DOWN TO WORK!

SUMÁRIO

Unit 1 – Do you know these celebrations?

Chapter 1	Let's practice – Festivals, celebrations, and holidays	8
	Telling dates	9
	Let's listen n' speak – April Fool's Day	10
Chapter 2	Language piece – Say × Tell × Speak × Talk	11
	Reported Speech	12
	Let's listen n' speak – Halloween	13
	Language piece – Time expressions	14
	Vocabulary hint – Common Pronunciation Problems: consoants	14
Chapter 3	Let's read n' write – Article: St. Patrick's Festival	15 a 17
Chapter 4	Tying in – World Festivals You won't Want To Miss	18
	Project – Brazilian Festivals	19

Unit 2 – What sport is tougher?

Chapter 1	Let's practice – Sports and sport's gadgets	22 e 23
	Let's listen n' speak – Sports influences	24
Chapter 2	Language piece – Comparisons: Equality	25
	Comparisons: Comparative	26
	Comparisons: Superlative	27
	Vocabulary hint – Comparisons' short adjective sounds	27
	Let's listen n' speak – Best players	28
Chapter 3	Let's read n' write – Interview: Teenager Mallory Pugh is the Future of Women's Soccer	29 a 31
Chapter 4	Citizenship moment – The Paralympic Games	32
	Project – Brazilian Paralympic Athletes	33

Review	34 e 35
Do not forget!	36
Overcoming challenges	37

Unit 3 – Have you ever done any of these things?

Chapter 1	Let's practice – Life experiences	40 e 41
	Let's listen n' speak – Bizarre food	42
Chapter 2	Language piece – Present Perfect (Regular verbs)	43 a 45
	Vocabulary hint – Contractions	45
	Let's listen n' speak – Riddle	46
Chapter 3	Let's read n' write – Travel blog – Ko Lipe: The Greatest Month in All My Travels	47 a 49
Chapter 4	Tying in – 10 Facts about indigenous aboriginal art and culture!	50
	Project – Original Inhabitants	51

Unit 4 – Have you ever done volunteer work?

Chapter 1	Let's practice – Types of volunteer work	54
	Language piece – Present Perfect (For × Since / Ever × Never)	55 e 56
	Let's listen n' speak – Charitable celebrities	56
Chapter 2	Language piece – Present Perfect (Irregular verbs)	57 a 59
	Adverbs (Never / Ever / Already / Yet)	58
	Vocabulary hint – Word stress	58
	Let's listen n' speak – Petsmart Charities	60
Chapter 3	Let's read n' write – Charity Campaign	61 a 63
Chapter 4	Citizenship moment – Five Benefits of Volunteering	64
	Project – Our Community	65

Review	66 e 67
Do not forget!	68
Overcoming challenges	69

Unit 5 – Have you ever heard about these places?

Chapter 1	**Let's practice** – Country's landmarks	**72 e 73**
	Big numbers	**73**
	Let's listen n' speak – Time machine	**74**
Chapter 2	**Language piece** – Simple Past × Present Perfect	**75**
	Ago × For	**76**
	Vocabulary hint – Contractions	**76**
	Let's listen n' speak – Places I have visited	**78**
Chapter 3	Let's read n' write – India Travel Guide	**79 a 81**
Chapter 4	**Citizenship moment** – Guide to greeting people around the world	**82**
	Project – Greeting etiquette	**83**

Unit 6 – How can they be described?

Chapter 1	**Let's practice** – Personality traits	**86 e 87**
	Let's listen n' speak – Personality traits	**88**
Chapter 2	**Language piece** – Adjective Ending: -ED × -ING	**89**
	Vocabulary hint – ED × -ING	**90**
	Relative pronouns	**91**
	Let's listen n' speak – Margalit's *Bat Mitzvah*	**92**
Chapter 3	**Let's read n' write** – Game profile: Creating an avatar	**93 a 95**
Chapter 4	**Tying in** – What is the Golden Rule?	**96**
	Project – Golden Rule: Try it out	**97**

Review	**98 e 99**
Do not forget!	**100**
Overcoming challenges	**101**

Unit 7 – What career would you choose?

Chapter 1	**Let's practice** – Job and professions	**104**
	Professions' gadgets	**105**
	Let's listen n' speak – Career fields	**106**
Chapter 2	**Language piece** – Infinitive × gerund	**107 a 109**
	Vocabulary hint – Short *to*	**108**
	Let's listen n' speak – Dream career	**110**
Chapter 3	**Let's read n' write** – Classified ads: Jobs	**111 a 113**
Chapter 4	**Tying in** – Introduction to knowing it's important	**114**
	Project – My résumé	**115**

Unit 8 – What about your health habits?

Chapter 1	**Let's practice** – Good habits × Bad habits	**118**
	Food groups	**119**
	Let's listen n' speak – Tips on health habits	**120**
Chapter 2	**Language piece** – Modal verbs: can and Should	**121**
	Countable and uncountable nouns: graded quantifiers	**122**
	Vocabulary hint – The *f* sound	**122**
	Let's listen n' speak – Nutricionist's prescription	**123 e 124**
Chapter 3	**Let's read n' write** – Food labels nutritional information	**125 a 127**
Chapter 4	**Citizenship moment** – Reducing Food Waste	**128**
	Project – Fighting food waste	**129**

Review	**130 e 131**
Do not forget!	**132**
Overcoming challenges	**133**

Workbook	**134 a 149**
Expert's point	**150 a 153**
20 Best Travel Tips After 20 Years of Traveling	**150 e 151**
Creating Healthy Habits	**152 e 153**

Focus on culture	**154 a 157**
Volunteering	**154 e 155**
Healthy Eating Habits	**156 e 157**
Language court	**158 a 171**
Glossary	**172 a 176**

UNIT 1
DO YOU KNOW THESE CELEBRATIONS?

_____

_____

_____

||| Get ready |||

1 What celebrations are these? Write the name of each celebration below its corresponding image.

> Carnival • Chinese New Year
> Day of the Dead / Día de los Muertos • Saint Patrick's Day

2 Are any of these celebrations traditional in your country?

_____
_____

3 What do you know about these celebrations? If you don't know anything, can you imagine what they are about?

_____
_____

4 What do these pictures have in common?

_____
_____

_____

CHAPTER 1

Let's practice

1 Think about Brazilian celebrations and answer the questions.

a) What do you usually celebrate throughout the year in your country?

_____

_____

b) Do you know the origins and the reasons why we celebrate certain commemorative dates?

_____

_____

c) Are there street parties in any of these traditional celebrations? Which ones?

_____

_____

2 Read the text about the UK and do what is asked.

CELEBRATIONS

Festivals, celebrations and public holidays

There are lots of events you can **get involved** with in the UK, from street parties to traditional holidays! Take a look at some of them.

January

1st – New Year's Day

On New Year's Eve (31st December), it is traditional to celebrate **midnight** with your friends or family. The party can last well into New Year's Day! Many people make 'New Year's resolutions', promising to achieve a goal or break a bad habit in the coming year. In Scotland, the celebration of the New Year is called Hogmanay.

March

17th – St. Patrick's Day (Northern Ireland)

The **Feast** of St. Patrick is a national holiday in Ireland, and is now celebrated by Irish communities all around the world.

April

Easter

Easter is a Christian holiday celebrating the **resurrection** of Jesus Christ. It is always on a Sunday in March or April. People celebrate Easter in different ways, but many give each other chocolate **Easter eggs**.

October

31st – Halloween

The modern way of celebrating Halloween is based on the Christian feast of All Hallows' Eve and the Celtic festival of Samhain. Children go **trick-or-treating** (knocking on neighbors' doors to ask for sweets) or **carve** pumpkins, while older students go to parties and Halloween events at pubs, clubs or Students' Unions – the important thing is to dress up as **gruesomely** as you dare!

December

Hanukkah

Jewish communities across the UK celebrate Hanukkah (Chanukah), the Festival of Lights, during eight days.

25th – Christmas

Most people in the UK celebrate Christmas, even if they are not **religious**. There will be Christmas trees, presents, **carol singing**, and if it snows, **snowmen** and **snowball fights**!

> **GLOSSARY**
>
> **Carol singing:** cânticos de natal.
> **Carve (to carve):** esculpir (esculpir).
> **Easter eggs:** ovos de páscoa.
> **Feast:** banquete.
> **Get involved (to get involved):** participar, envolver-se (envolver-se).
> **Gruesomely:** de forma horrível, repulsiva.
> **Midnight:** meia-noite.
> **Religious:** religioso.
> **Resurrection:** ressurreição.
> **Snowball fight:** guerra de bolas de neve.
> **Snowmen:** bonecos de neve.
> **Trick-or-treating:** gostosuras ou travessuras.

Based on: British Council. *Holiday and festival calendar.* Available at: <https://study-uk.britishcouncil.org/living/holidays-festivals-events>. Access: June 2017.

a) Complete with the correct date of celebration in the United Kingdom.

- New Year's Day: _____.
- Easter: _____.
- St. Patrick's Day: _____.
- Halloween: _____.
- Christmas: _____.

b) Which of these celebrations do you have in your country? Are they celebrated on the same date?

_____

_____

c) Do you celebrate any of the mentioned holidays? Do you do anything special? Copy the following table on your notebook, complete it, and share your answers with a partner.

Holiday	Travel	Gifts	Special Food	Party / Parade / Ceremony

Let's listen n' speak

1 **Discuss with your classmates.**

a) Are there any funny dates that are usually celebrated, even though they are not a holiday?

b) What do you know about this day? What is really celebrated on this date?

2 **Listen to Mark and Clara and answer the questions.**

a) What are they talking about?

- ( ) April Fool's Day.
- ( ) New Year's Day.

b) What was the reason this date began to be celebrated?

- ( ) A change on Christmas' Day.
- ( ) A change in the Christian calendar.

c) Was this change something easily spread? Why?

_____
_____

d) What did people start to do to the ones who forgot that the date changed?

_____
_____

3 **Mark the sentences with T (true) or F (false).**

- ( ) April Fool's Day began due to a communication problem.
- ( ) New Year was celebrated on April 1st in medieval France.
- ( ) Everybody understood the change in New Year's celebration date.
- ( ) People who didn't know about the New Year's new celebration date were called smart.

4 **Pair up and tell your partner the false sentences from the previous exercise making them true.**

_____
_____
_____
_____

Let's practice

 1 **Do you know the difference between to say, to tell, to talk and to speak? Circle the best alternative to complete each sentence.**

a) He (said / told) me that he couldn't go to the party.

b) Mom (said / told) that she was sorry for being late to pick us up at school.

c) We (talked / spoke) about our vacation plans.

d) Did she (speak / talk) to you about the reorganization plans?

> **LANGUAGE PIECE**
>
> **To say:** to speak words (something) to somebody.
>
> **To tell:** to give information to a person.
>
> **To talk:** to converse with another person about something.
>
> **To speak:** to say something using your voice, to take some monologues / serious conversation or to refer to the knowledge of other languages.

 2 **Complete the story using the correct form of say or tell.**

Yoko: Karen, I need to _____ you something about George.

Yoko: Yesterday morning he talked to me about you. He really likes you and he _____ he was going to speak to you about his feelings.

Karen: I know! We talked yesterday while coming back home from school. He _____ me he wanted to be my date at the prom!

Yoko: Really?! What did you _____?

Karen: I couldn't _____ anything, I just nodded yes!

3 Rewrite the sentences using the reported speech.

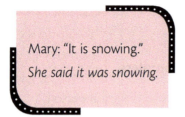

Mary: "It is snowing."
She said it was snowing.

LANGUAGE PIECE
Reported Speech
Also known as **indirect speech**.
Direct Speech ⟶ Reported Speech
Present tenses ⟶ Past tenses

a) Simone: "My brother is making some cookies."

_____

b) "There will be a test tomorrow", the teacher said to the students.

_____

c) "They are building a bridge here", said the engineer.

_____

d) "We have written one hundred pages", Amelia told the editor.

_____

4 Read the pair of sentences and circle the correct one.

a) Omar said he was traveling that day. / Omar told he was traveling that day.

b) Laura said her mother were sick. / Laura said her mother had been sick.

c) The children told their parents they can swim. / The children told their parents they could swim.

d) Vlad told Ivan his mother had made a cake the day before. / Vlad told Ivan his mother has made a cake the day before.

e) Francesca said her would bring a salad the week after. / Francesca said she would bring a salad the week after.

5 All sentences have a mistake. Circle it and rewrite the sentence correctly.

a) She said it were cold.

_____

b) The explorer saying they had found gold here.

_____

c) The boys tell the teacher they would travel.

_____

Let's listen n' speak

TRACK 02

1 **What celebration is Arjun telling his family about? Circle it.**

a)
GTS Productions/Shutterstock.com

b)
Zuma Press/Easypix Brasil

c)
Ryan McVay/Getty Images

2 **What words do not relate to what was said...**

a) ... about Halloween?

- ◯ boring
- ◯ nice
- ◯ difficult

b) ... about the place they usually meet?

- ◯ behind the house
- ◯ at the cafeteria
- ◯ in front of the house

c) ... about the candy they get?

- ◯ gummy bears
- ◯ ice cream
- ◯ apple pie

d) ... about what Aaron takes before he starts?

- ◯ a nap
- ◯ a shower
- ◯ a photo

e) ... about what they do when they get to a house?

- ◯ ring the bell
- ◯ knock
- ◯ shout

3 **Listen again and answer the questions about Arjun's.**

a) What does Aaron do after he puts on his costume?

_____

b) What costume does he wear?

_____

c) What do the boys do after they pick up the baskets?

_____

d) When do kids normally get candy?

_____

13

Let's practice

1) Complete with the correct option.

a) _____ Doug finishes his homework, he will go to the cinema. (before / after)

b) David called an ambulance _____ he saw the accident. (before / when)

c) Please call us _____ you arrive at the hotel. (when / before)

d) _____ I am at home, I rest on my sofa. (when / before)

e) Alison checks the address _____ she drives somewhere new. (before / after)

2) Complete the sentences with when, before or after.

a) I had breakfast _____ I brushed my teeth.

b) _____ I am older I want to travel the world.

c) We ate breakfast _____ we made the pancakes.

LANGUAGE PIECE

Time expressions
Connect two actions / events at a point of time.
When a period of time; at an specific time.
Before earlier than an specific event.
After later than an specific event.

3) Organize the words in one sentence by adding when, before or after.

a) Lucy / went to bed / brushed her teeth.

_____

b) Bob / bought tickets / enter the cinema.

_____

c) Bob / paid for dinner / found his wallet.

_____

d) I / have no idea / the party will start.

_____

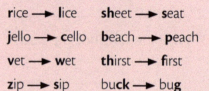

Vocabulary hint
Common Pronunciation Problems: Consonants

rice → lice   sheet → seat
jello → cello   beach → peach
vet → wet   thirst → first
zip → sip   buck → bug

4) Match the uses.

a) When

b) Before

c) After

• Indicates a posterior period of time.

• Indicates a period of time.

• Indicates an early period of time.

14

Let's read n' write

1) What festive dates do you usually celebrate throughout the year in your country?

_____

_____

2) Do you know the origins and the reasons why we celebrate certain commemorative dates? Talk about them with your classmates.

3) Are there street parties in any of these traditional celebrations to make people get involved? Which ones? Talk about them with your classmates.

4) Read this article about an interesting Irish holiday and answer the questions about it.

Tourism and Culture

St. Patrick's Festival

Celebrate Ireland's national holiday – the day when everybody is a little **bit** Irish! Saint Patrick's Day is a cultural and religious holiday celebrated on 17th March, the anniversary of his **death**.

Patryk Kosmider/Shutterstock.com

It commemorates Saint Patrick (c. A.D. 387-461), the most **commonly recognised** of the **patron saints** of Ireland and the arrival of Christianity in Ireland. Saint Patrick's Day was made an official **feast** day in the **early** seventeenth century and has **gradually become** a celebration of Irish culture in general. It is a public holiday in the Republic of Ireland but it is also **widely** celebrated by the Irish Diaspora **across** the globe making it the most celebrated saints day in the world. Dublin is the **host** of the **largest** parade in Ireland with over 3,000 performers and on average 500,000 people **attending**. In addition to the **legendary** parade, which **immerses** the city centre in a carnival atmosphere, the festival is **bursting at the seams** with music, dance, culture, family fun and more!

Irish Tourism. *St. Patricks Festival*. Available at: <www.irishtourism.com/festivals-in-ireland/st-patricks-festival/1309>. Access: Feb. 2018.

GLOSSARY

Across: através.
Attending (to attend): participando (participar).
Become (to become): tornou-se (tornar-se).
Bit: um pouco.
Bursting at the seams (slang): lugar que abriga um grande número de pessoas ou coisas, excessivamente lotado (gíria).
Celebrate (to celebrate): comemore (comemorar).
Commonly: comumente.
Death: morte.
Early: no começo.
Feast: banquete, celebração.
Gradually: gradualmente.
Host (to host): hospeda / abriga (hospedar / abrigar).
Immerses (to immerse): mergulha / imerge (mergulhar / imergir).
Largest: maior.
Legendary: lendário.
Patron: patrono.
Recognised (to recognise): reconhecido (reconhecer).
Saints: santos.
Widely: amplamente.

a) When is St. Patrick's Day celebrated?

_____

b) When was St. Patrick's Day made an official feast?

_____

c) Which city hosts the largest Saint Patrick's parade?

_____

5 **Mark T (true) or F (false).**

a) ( ) Saint Patrick is the most celebrated saint in the world.

b) ( ) Saint Paul is the most commonly recognized saint of Ireland.

c) ( ) _Diaspora_ means "migration of people".

d) ( ) Saint Patrick's Day is a public holiday in Ireland.

e) ( ) An average of 500 thousand performers present during the parade.

f) ( ) There isn't music, dance or fun in the festival.

6 **Analyze the text and answer.**

a) What kind of information does it show?

- ( ) Historical facts.
- ( ) Dates.
- ( ) Geographic aspects.

- ( ) Cultural traditions.
- ( ) World events.
- ( ) Specific locations.

b) What kind of text is it?

- ( ) Descriptive.
- ( ) Informative.
- ( ) Narrative.
- ( ) Persuasive.
- ( ) Review.

- ( ) Essay.
- ( ) News.
- ( ) Report.
- ( ) Pamphlet.
- ( ) Article.

c) Where can texts like this be found?

_____

7 Let's create an article about a Brazilian national holiday. Follow the instructions.

Think about the information it should have:
- When is it?
- Why is it celebrated?
- What is its history?
- Where is it celebrated?
- How is it celebrated?
- Is there any special fact about it?

Chapter 4

||| Tying in |||

Celebrations – Culture

World Festivals You Won't Want To Miss

Add them to your bucket list, because these are one in a lifetime.

By Ashly Perez

Snow & Ice Festival – Harbin, China

When: Jan. 5 TH – Feb. 5 TH
Where: Harbin, China
Why you should go: The Harbin festival is the largest snow and ice festival in the world, and it **features carvings towering** over 20 feet in height and **full-size** buildings made from gigantic blocks of ice.

Mardi Gras – New Orleans

When: Tuesday before Ash Wednesday […]
Where: New Orleans
Why you should go: In many ways Mardis Gras' reputation **precedes** itself – if you want to party like there's no tomorrow, New Orleans is where you belong. […]

Holi – Celebrated by Hindus Around the World

When: March 27 TH (for 2014)
Where: India, Nepal, Sri Lanka, and other Hindu regions
Why you should go: Holi, also known as the Festival of Colors, celebrates the end of winter and the beginning of spring. It's fun, safe, and free. Just remember to BYOD (bring your own **dye**). […]

Albuquerque International Balloon Festival – Albuquerque, N.M.

When: Oct. 5 TH-13 TH (for 2014)
Where: Albuquerque, N.M.
Why you should go: The Albuquerque International Balloon Festival is the largest **gathering** of hot-air balloons in the world. Essentially, it's like *Up* – but better. […]

GLOSSARY

Ablaze: em chamas.
Carvings: esculturas.
Costume: traje, fantasia.
Display: exibição.
Dye: corante, tinta.
Features: características.
Full-size: tamanho completo/real.
Gathering: reunião.
Held (to hold): mantido (manter).
Light up (to light up): acender, iluminar.
Passed (to pass): faleceu (falecer).
Precedes (to precede): precede (proceder).
Towering (to tower): elevando-se.

Celebrations – Culture

Día de los Muertos – Celebrated by Mexicans in the U.S., Canada, Europe and Mexico

When: Nov. 1 ST
Where: Celebrations are **held** by cultural Mexicans throughout the world [...]
Why you should go: Día de los Muertos, or "The Day of the Dead," celebrates All Saint's Day, which remembers all those who have **passed** before us. A colorful **display** of **costume** and culture, Día de los Muertos is a day you don't want to miss. [...]

Lantern Festival – Pingxi, Taiwan

When: Feb. 23 RD (for 2014)
Where: Pingxi, Taiwan
Why you should go: Watch the sky **light up** during one of the world's largest lantern festivals. If you're looking for a little magic, there is nothing more surreal than a sky **ablaze** with thousands of floating lanterns. [...]

Perez, Ashly. 23 *World festivals you won't want to miss.* BuzzFeed. Available at: <www.buzzfeed.com/ashleyperez/23-world-festivals-you-wont-want-to-miss?utm_term=.eimqDmRJn#.toLNADVRz>.
Access: June 2018.

 **Let's practice**

 EXPLORING

Coco, 2017.

1) What do these celebrations represent?

  a) Día de los Muertos
  b) Holi
  c) Lanter Festival
  d) Snow & Ice Festival

  • Reproduces buildings in full-size.
  • Celebrates the beginning of spring.
  • Remembers all those who are no longer alive.
  • The largest festival that light up the sky.

PROJECT

Brazilian Festivals

Organize yourselves into five groups. Each group will be responsible for looking for the festivals and celebrations of a specific Brazilian region. Gather all the interesting information and share it with the other groups, then decide on two festivals of each region to write about in a class informative.

2) What is your favorite festival from the text? Why? Talk about them with your classmates.

UNIT 2
WHAT SPORT IS TOUGHER?

||| Get ready |||

1 Which sports are these? How did you infer that?

- ◯ Basketball.
- ◯ Canoeing.
- ◯ Golf.
- ◯ Gymnastics.
- ◯ Karate.
- ◯ Judo.
- ◯ Mountain biking.
- ◯ Table tennis.
- ◯ Tennis.
- ◯ Running.
- ◯ Volleyball.
- ◯ Swimming.

2 Discuss with your classmates.

a) Do you know what an Adaptive Sport is?

b) Are any Adaptive Sports represented on the pictures? Which ones?

_____

c) Do you like sports? Which one / ones do you play? Talk with a classmate about it.

CHAPTER 1

Let's practice

1 Can you guess which sport it is? Look at the pictures and write the correct name under each one.

cycling • football • golf • gymnastics • soccer • surfing • tennis • volleyball

a)

stockphoto-graf/Shutterstock.com

_____

c)

supparsorn/Shutterstock.com

_____

e)

Kletr/Shutterstock.com

_____

g)

pukach/Shutterstock.com

_____

b)

Sergiy1975/Shutterstock.com

_____

d)

artproem/Shutterstock.com

_____

f)

jakkapan/Shutterstock.com

_____

h)

pukach/Shutterstock.com

_____

2 Go, do or play? Write the following sports under the correct verb net.

archery • athletics • baseball • basketball
canoeing • cycling • football • gymnastics
judo • running • soccer • swimming

Go

_____

_____

Play

_____

_____

_____

Do

_____

_____

Ilustrações: Marcos de Mello

3 Circle the correct word.

a) My brother runs faster when he wears…

bow.   sneakers.

d) Susanna didn't play tennis because she lost her…

racket.   sneakers.

b) When I go cycling I must wear a…

helmet.   goggles.

e) To practice archery you need a…

bow.   racket.

c) When people go canoeing, they need a good…

oar.   racket.

f) To go swimming, my mom wears a pair of…

sneakers.   goggles.

4 Match the sports equipment and its function.

a) Goggles
b) Helmets
c) Oars
d) Rackets
e) Sneakers
f) Bows

- Protect the head.
- Used to row a boat on water.
- Protect the eyes.
- Shoot arrows into air.
- Strike balls in games.
- Protect your feet.

Let's listen n' speak

1 Before listening to Jessica, answer the following questions orally.

a) Is there a national sport in Brazil?

b) Does everybody have the same opinions on sports, teams etc.?

c) Can you think of some adjectives that are used when talking about sports and teams?

2 Listen to Jessica talking about her sports influences and do what is asked.

a) What is Jessica's opinion about sports? _____

b) Did Jessica's parents encourage her to practice different sports? _____

c) Check all the sports Jessica practices.

- ◯ baseball
- ◯ gymnastics
- ◯ soccer
- ◯ tennis
- ◯ cycling
- ◯ basketball
- ◯ swimming
- ◯ volleyball

3 Let's talk about sports! Pair up and be creative. Write two more questions and use them in your conversations.

- What's your favorite sport? How often do you play it?
- In your opinion, what sport can be dangerous? Why?
- Which sport style do you prefer: team or individual?
- Which do you prefer: sports or computer games? Why?

EXPLORING
- *The Miracle Season*, 2018.
- *Queen of the Katwe*, 2016.
- *Race*, 2016.

CHAPTER 2

Let's practice

1 Read the dialogue between Barney and his son Samuel.

GLOSSARY
Bet (to bet): aposto (apostar).
Long face (slang): triste, desapontado (gíria).

a) Samuel considers his team to be:
- ◯ good.
- ◯ bad.
- ◯ very bad.

b) What did Barney mean when he said: "Oh, I'll bet it's not **as bad as** all that!"?
- ◯ His son's team is bad.
- ◯ His son's team is not so bad.
- ◯ His son's team is good.

2 Complete the sentences with the correct comparative form of the adjectives.

a) Look at those swimmers! Wow! The Brazilian is _____ the Chinese! (fast)

b) Cameron's soccer team has trained _____ all the other teams. (hard)

c) In my opinion, Rio's opening ceremony was _____ London's. (beautiful)

d) I don't want to watch this game. It is _____ doing nothing! (boring)

3 Complete the sentences with the appropriate adjective.

> heavy • interesting • long • old • popular • rich

a) American football players are as _____ as Brazilian soccer players.

b) Weightlifters are as _____ as Sumo wrestlers.

c) In Brazil, volleyball is as _____ as swimming.

d) The board game Senet is as _____ as the board game Royal Game of Ur.

LANGUAGE PIECE

Equality
Use **as adjective as**.
Express comparisons when things are equal in some way.

4 Adeline is taking a gym class.

GLOSSARY

Faster (fast): mais rápido.

Push (to push): dá uma forçada (forçar).

a) What sport is she practicing? _____

b) When the coach says "**C'mon, faster!**" it means Adeline should:

- ◯ increase the speed.
- ◯ decrease the speed.
- ◯ maintain the speed.

LANGUAGE PIECE

Comparative

Use **adjective** + **(-er) than** or **more adjective than**.

Compare two things, people, places etc.

5 Circle the correct answer.

a) Look at those women in track and field! Wow! The Russian is _____ the Japanese! (more taller than / taller than)

b) Italy's soccer is _____ Portugal's soccer. Turn off the TV. (more boring than / boring than)

c) In my opinion, Tokyo's opening ceremony will be _____ London's. (cheaper than / more cheap than)

d) I do not want to watch this game. Greg Hardy is _____ Jonathan Dwyer. (more strong than / stronger than)

6 Rewrite the sentences with the opposite comparative.

a) Usain Bolt is more famous than Christopher Taylor.

_____

b) Uncas Talles had a better performance than Alexis Garcia in rowing.

_____

c) Thiago Braz jumped higher than Renaud Lavillenie in men's pole vault.

_____

7 Taylor got mail.

GLOSSARY
Award: prêmio.
Comeback: retorno.
Injured: ferido(a).
Made (to make): fez (fazer).

a) What is the mail about? _____

b) Who do they give this award to?
- ◯ To injured athletes who returned to sports.
- ◯ To injured athletes who retired from sports.

c) How should the athlete's comeback be in order to win the award?
- ◯ Average.
- ◯ Exceptional.
- ◯ Good.

Vocabulary hint
Comparison's short adjective sounds
long   lon**ger**   lon**gest**
strong stron**ger** stron**gest**
young   youn**ger**   youn**gest**

8 Write the correct superlative forms of the adjectives.

a) important: _____

b) slow: _____

c) famous: _____

d) competitive: _____

e) good: _____

f) different: _____

LANGUAGE PIECE
Superlative
Use **the adjective** + (**-est**) or **the most adjective**.
Express comparisons when there are three or more elements or references.

9 Answer with full sentences.

a) Who is the oldest person in your class?
_____

b) Who is the tallest person in your family?
_____

c) What is the hardest exercise you have done today?
_____

d) In your opinion, what is the most difficult sport?
_____

Let's listen n' speak

1 Listen to Malina and Kieran first meeting and answer the questions.

a) What sport are they playing? _____

b) How long has Malina lived in that area so far?
_____

c) In Kieran's opinion, how many times is Durant better than LeBron?
- ◯ 10.
- ◯ 100.
- ◯ 1,000.

d) Who is Malina's father?
- ◯ Stephen Curry.
- ◯ Bogdan Bogdanovic.
- ◯ Rick Rubio.

2 Add the missing words and then put them in order.

a) is / than / you / Durant / better / do / think / _____ ?
_____

b) Serbia / _____ / player / in / dad / my / back / is.
_____

c) _____ / Stephen Curry / as / is / LeBron James / good.
_____

d) worse / _____ / than / the / is / Rick Rubio.
_____

3 Let's talk a little bit more about sports.

- What are the most popular sports in Brazil?
- Can you name some famous players of your favorite sport?
- Is there any sports center near your home or school? Do you usually go there?
- Which do you prefer: watching or playing sports? Why?
- Can you explain any sports rules?
- In your opinion, who is the best and the worst sports player?

Let's practice

1 Mallory Pugh is a young soccer player. Read her interview.

SPORTS ILLUSTRATED KIDS

Teenager Mallory Pugh is the Future of Women's Soccer

Hollis Belger | February 22nd 2016, 9:06 am

Like a lot of 17 year olds, Mallory Pugh loves playing sports. But **unlike** her high school friends, the team Mallory plays for is the United States.

As captain of the US Women's National Team **U-20 squad**, Mallory is the youngest player to take the field for the USWNT since 2005 and the youngest **to score** a goal in the past 16 years.

[...] Mallory spoke with SI Kids about her experience playing for the United States, balancing school and sports, and who her soccer role models are.

How does it feel right now to be playing at the highest level of soccer in our country at such a young age?

I think it's a really great honor to be playing at the highest level at 17. I think without the support of my friends and family I definitely wouldn't be here. But, again, I think it's a **once-in-a-lifetime** opportunity, and I'm just trying **to take it all in**.

Is it difficult to keep up with your friends and your "normal" life, like school and hanging out with friends, while you're so busy with soccer? If so, how does that make you feel?

Sometimes, obviously, I'll **miss out** on going to a school basketball game or whatever and I'll get upset, but I know that being here with the national team is such a great opportunity. All my friends know that. I think they're just super happy for me, which makes going away from home a little easier.

When did you start playing soccer?
I started playing when I was four!

When do you think you really started standing out as a special player?
I would maybe say when I was U13, so like 12 or 13 years old, that I went to a tournament with my older team, and I think that's when I mainly and seriously got scouted.

When did you know that this was what you wanted to do with your life, to play soccer professionally?
I think ever since I was little — maybe 9 or 10 — I've always just had a dream. I think once I started getting invited to youth national team camps, that's when I really started saying, "Maybe this is possible. Maybe this is something I can do." I think my first camp I was around 13 or 14. [...]

Did you ever have other passions that you had to put aside in order to pursue competitive soccer?
I played basketball. I wasn't really a fan of basketball too much, but I really liked doing track and field, too. Deep down, whenever I go in the summer time to Beaver Lake, I play beach volleyball, and I've always wished I could do that.
[...]

What would you say to young girls who aspire to be the best they can be in their sport, whether it's soccer or another sport?
When I was young, I think one thing that really took a toll on me was knowing if I was able to be there. I think just gaining your confidence through your play and through your friendships with your teammates is really key at such a young age. I think another thing would just be to stay dedicated and motivated for whatever you want to do, because you never know what can happen!
[...]

Sports illustrated kids. Available at: <www.sikids.com/si-kids/2016/02/22/teenager-mallory-pugh-future-womens-soccer>. Access: June 2018.

a) Discuss with your classmates: How many teenagers do you know at pro leagues?

2) Read the interview again and answer the questions.

a) Who is Mallory Pugh?
_____
_____

b) How long had passed since the last youngest player had scored at the USNT?
_____
_____

c) How does Mallory feel about being part of a professional soccer team?

- ◯ She feels distressed.
- ◯ She feels enthusiastic.
- ◯ She feels conventional.

GLOSSARY

Hanging out (to hang out): saindo com alguém (sair com alguém).
Miss out (to miss out): perder.
Once-in-a-lifetime: uma vez na vida.
Scouted: termo usado em esportes para observar talentos promissores.
Standing out (to stand out): destacou-se (destacar-se).
To keep up with: acompanhar, estar a par de.
To put aside: pôr de lado.
To score: pontuar.
To take it all in: assimilar.
Took a toll on: expressão idiomática que remete a algo que causa sofrimento.
U-20 squad: time Sub-20.
Unlike: ao contrário.

d) How do Mallory's friends face her life as a professional soccer player?

- ( ) Her friends are supportive.

- ( ) Her friends are envious.

e) When does Mallory think she started to stand out?

_____

f) How old was Mallory when she got invited to her first national team camp?

_____

g) What other sports does Mallory enjoy?

_____

h) What is Mallory's advice to the young people pursuing a sports career?

_____

(3) Think about the text and its characteristics and answer the questions.

a) What kind of text is it? _____

b) Who is the text for? _____

c) What is the purpose of the text? _____

d) What kind of language is used in it? Give examples.

_____

_____

e) What elements are part of this type of text?

_____

(4) Go back to item a from exercise 1. Choose one of the young sportspeople you talked about and do as it follows using your notebook.

a) Make a list of questions you would like to ask this person.

b) Research this person and try to gather the answers to your questions.

c) Write an interview article using all the data you collected.

d) Exchange compositions with a partner and correct it.

e) Rewrite your article observing the corrections done and hand it in.

||| Citizenship moment |||

The Paralympic Games
Kids Encyclopedia

INTRODUCTION

The Paralympic Games are a major international sports event for people with **disabilities**. The name Paralympics means "**alongside** the Olympics" and the athletes are called Paralympians. These games **take place** after the Olympic Games, in the same city.

HISTORY

The Paralympics can be **traced back** to 1948, when a doctor named Ludwig Guttmann organized a small athletic **gathering** in the United Kingdom for British World War II veterans, in the same day as the opening ceremony of the Summer Olympics in London.

The first Paralympic Games were held in 1960 in Rome. There are Winter and Summer Paralympic Games that are held just after the Olympic Games. All Paralympic Games are governed by the International Paralympic Committee (IPC).

ATHLETES

Athletes from countries all around the world compete in the Paralympics. This includes athletes with mobility disabilities, amputations, blindness, and Cerebral **Palsy**.

Some have **spinal cord injuries** and missing **limbs**, and they may use **wheelchairs** or prostheses (artificial limbs) to move around. Some have muscular dystrophy or other conditions that limit movement. Some are blind or have limited vision. Others have cerebral palsy or intellectual (mental) disabilities.

Paralympians work for equal treatment with **able-bodied** Olympic athletes who receive much more financial support than Paralympic athletes.

ORGANIZATION

The International Paralympic Committee (IPC) has organized The Paralympic Games since 1989 and it is based in Germany. One of its goals is to help athletes with disabilities achieve excellence in sports. Another goal is to increase the world's respect and admiration for people with disabilities.

EVENTS

There are the Summer Paralympic Games, where participants compete in more than a dozen sports, **such as** archery, track and field, cycling, **rowing**, table tennis, wheelchair, basketball and many others. At the Winter Paralympic Games, athletes compete in **ice sledge**, hockey, skiing, and other cold-weather sports.

Sources: *Kiddle encyclopedia*. Available at: <https://kids.kiddle.co/Paralympic_Games>; *Britannica Kids*, available at: <https://kids.britannica.com/kids/article/Paralympic-Games/599583/306984-toc>. Access: Feb. 2018.

GLOSSARY

Able-bodied: sem deficiência física.
Alongside: junto com.
Disabilities: deficiências.
Gathering: reunião/encontro.
Ice sledge: trenó de gelo.
Limbs: membros do corpo.
Palsy: paralisia.
Rowing: remo.
Spinal cord injuries: lesões da medula espinhal.
Such as: tal como.
Take place (to take place): acontece (acontecer).
Traced back (to trace back): remete (remeter).
Wheelchairs: cadeira de rodas.

Let's practice

1 What are the Paralympic Games?

_____

2 What does the name Paralympics mean?

a) ◯ Parallel with the Olympics.

b) ◯ Superior to the Olympics.

3 Who organized the first athletic reunion for disabled war veterans?

EXPLORING
- 23 Blast, 2014.
- Where Hope Grows, 2014.
- No Ordinary Hero: The SuperDeafy Movie, 2013.

_____

4 When did the first Paralympic Games happen?

a) ◯ In 1948.   b) ◯ In 1960.   c) ◯ In 1968.

5 What is the abbreviation for the institution that rules the Paralympic Games?

a) ◯ ICP.   b) ◯ IPG.   c) ◯ IPC.

6 What kinds of disabilities do the Paralympic Games include?

_____
_____

7 What are The International Paralympic Committee goals?

_____
_____
_____
_____

PROJECT

Brazilian Paralympic Athletes

Organize yourselves into five groups and research the Brazilian Paralympic athletes and the institutions that support them. Look for all the information you can find related to their access to sports practices, financial support, official institutes, and challenges they face.

After the research, gather all the information all the groups found out and make an informative infographic with the most important findings.

33

REVIEW

1) Unscramble the words to form sentences.

a) a / ago / Dimitri / us / many / told / lie / years / horrible.

b) to / tell / you / go / me / can / where / ?

c) accident / telling / why / everything / the / aren't / me / you / about /?

d) wait / said / here, / the / boss.

2) Rewrite the sentences into reported speech.

a) "My mother is sick", Mario told Vanessa.

b) "They were making fire in the woods last month", said Simone.

c) "Hans has driven carefully this week", Amelia told the supervisor.

d) "I will call you if I have a chance", Lisa explained to her friend.

e) "Our dad takes us to school", said the children.

3) Read the pairs of sentences and choose the correct one.

a) ◯ Luna said she was traveling tomorrow.
   ◯ Luna told them she was traveling that day.

b) ◯ Aaron said he mother was sick.
   ◯ Aaron said his mother had been sick.

4 **Answer with true answers for you.**

a) What is as difficult as Math?

_____

b) What city is as beautiful as your city?

_____

c) What sport is as popular as soccer?

_____

d) Who is not as fast as Usain Bolt?

_____

e) Which Olympic Games were as exciting as Rio's?

_____

5 **Write sentences comparing the sports.**

a) gymnastics × judo: _____

b) swimming × archery: _____

c) fencing × skiing: _____

d) baseball × soccer: _____

6 **Find the mistake and circle it. Then rewrite the sentence correctly.**

a) This book is interestingest in the library.

_____

b) My brother is more bad at tennis in my family.

_____

c) The cheetah is the most fast animal among felines.

_____

d) The blue whale is the heavyest animal in the water.

_____

DO NOT FORGET!

ORAL COMMUNICATION

TO SPEAK/SPOKE
Monologue, serious conversation, language knowledge

TO TALK/TALKED
To converse with another person about something

TO TELL/TOLD
To give information to a person about something

TO SAY/SAID
To speak words (something) to somebody

REPORTED SPEECH: reproduces another person's speech / what another person has said.

EXAMPLE:
Megan: "I'm happy today."
Me: Megan told me she was happy that day.

ORIGINAL SENTENCE	REPORTED SPEECH
Simple Present	Simple Past
Present Continuous	Past Continuous
Simple Past	Past Perfect

WHEN do people **celebrate** Carnival?

BEFORE: preceding moment/period
People celebrate Carnival on February, before March.

Asks or refers to a specific moment in time.

CELEBRATIONS: Carnival / Chinese New Year / Día de Los Muertos / St. Patrick's Day / April Fool's Day / Christmas / New Year

AFTER: following moment / period
People celebrate Carnival on February, **after** January.

VERBS
Go Play Do

SPORTS WITH 'DO' archery / athletics / gymnastics / judo / karate

SPORTS WITH 'PLAY' baseball / basketball / football / golf / table tennis / tennis / volleyball

SPORTS WITH 'GO' swimming / canoeing / cycling / running / surfing / mountain biking

COMPARATIVES AND SUPERLATIVES

EQUALITY

AS + ADJECTIVE + AS

My sister is **as tall as** me. We're both 1.65.

SUPERIORITY Short adjectives

ADJECTIVE + ER THAN

My sister is **taller than** me.

SUPERIORITY Long adjectives

MORE + ADJECTIVE THAN

My sister is **more beautiful** than me.

SUPERLATIVE Short adjectives

ADJECTIVE + EST

My sister is the **tallest** girl in the family.

SUPERLATIVE Long adjectives

THE MOST + ADJECTIVE

My sister is the **most beautiful** girl.

OVERCOMING CHALLENGES

(PUC)

Papyrus was used _____ than paper.

a) early

b) earlier

c) more early

d) earlyer

e) earliest

The "Herald" is _____ newspaper in the town.

a) the importantest

b) the more important

c) the less important

d) the most important

e) the importanter

(FMU)

That table is _____ than this one.

a) long

b) more long

c) longest

d) longer

e) most long

UNIT 3
HAVE YOU EVER DONE ANY OF THESE THINGS?

||| Get ready |||

1 Do you know any of these activities? Try to match the images to the names from the box.

> baking • dying hair • painting
> rock climbing • tattooing • traveling abroad

2 Have you ever tried any of these activities? If not, which one would you like to try?

3 Fill in the blanks with the verbs below.

> baked • dyed • painted
> rock climbed • tattooed • traveled

a) My brother has never _____ his hair, it has always been blond.

b) I have never _____ because I don't like high places.

c) My brother has _____ my birthday cake, isn't it amazing?

d) My neighbor has _____ a dragon on his arm.

e) My parents have never _____ abroad.

f) Our cousin has _____ a very beautiful scene on our bedroom wall.

CHAPTER 1

Let's practice

1 Write the correct heading to each chatroom post.

Exciting sports • Exotic food • Going to places • Image change

Life Experiences

Unusual experiences

Sakura, 12
I'm from Japan and my family loves to travel. They've taken me to some places like the United States, South Africa, Uruguay and Spain.

Peter, 11
I'm a Hungarian boy who has been to many countries in Europe, like France, England, Ireland, and Switzerland, but I've never been to Budapest.

Karen, 13
I've dyed my hair several times. It's been red, purple, dark blue, and orange. Right now it is light pink.

John, 15
I've never tattooed my body, but I've considered doing it as soon as I turn 21 years old.

Richard, 18
I've always loved to try new and different foods. I've tried fried spiders, cooked snakes, and frogs.

Margo, 14
My parents and I have been in a jungle expedition once. Then, we tried toasted bugs and fried spiders.

Maria, 17
I have always loved extreme sports, such as bungee jumping, and the like. I've already gone rock climbing and skydiving.

Arthur, 14
I've been skiing and snowboarding a lot of times.

2. Answer the questions.

a) Who has already gone to Uruguay?

_____

b) Who has already eaten cooked snakes?

_____

c) Who has a pierced nose?

_____

d) Who has gone rock climbing?

_____

3. Read the chatroom posts again and write T (true) or F (false).

a) ◯ John has got a pierced nose and a tattoo.

b) ◯ Sakura has already been to Vietnam.

c) ◯ Margo has eaten toasted bugs.

d) ◯ Peter has never been to Budapest.

e) ◯ Richard has already eaten bugs.

f) ◯ Arthur has gone rafting several times.

g) ◯ Karen has dyed her hair many times by now.

h) ◯ Maria has never done scuba diving.

4. Match the pictures to the words below.

arrive • bump into • cook • laugh • spill • talk • try on • watch

a) c) e) g)

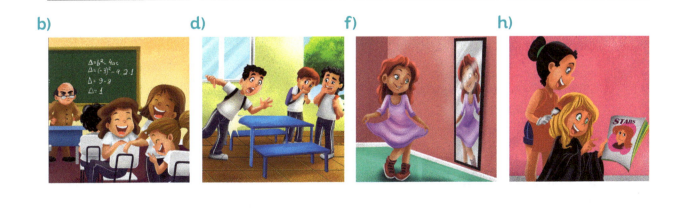

b) d) f) h)

Let's listen n' speak

1 Listen to the radio interview program and answer the questions.

a) Why does he eat things such as brain and bugs?
_____

b) What is the name of the show?
- ( ) Bizarre Moments.
- ( ) Fantastic Foods.
- ( ) Bizarre Foods.

c) In his opinion, what is the goal of the show?
_____
_____

d) What is the reason he started the show?
_____

2 Work in pairs and analyze the following ad.

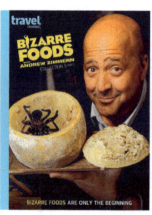

Travel Channel

a) Describe the food on this ad. What is different about this food?
_____
_____

b) Is there in your country any traditional dish that may be strange for other people?
_____
_____

c) Have you ever tried any of these traditional dishes from your country? Use the prompts below and talk to a partner about it.

- When do people typically eat this food? Is it part of the daily diet or a dish for special occasions?
- Have people's eating habits changed in your country? How?
- Is there a difference between what people eat in the cities and in the rural areas?
- Are there any foods you don't like?
- Is there a food you haven't tried yet but would like to try?

42

Let's practice

1 **Look at the following sentences.**

> Get to know food you've never heard about!
> Find out about a different food experience you haven't tasted yet!

LANGUAGE PIECE

Present Perfect – Regular verbs

Present Perfect – actions that happened at an **unspecified** time before now.

a) Circle the main verbs in the sentences.

b) Organize the verbs into the correct category.

Infinitive form	Past participle form

c) Which verb appears in both sentences? And which is its function in the sentence: **main** or **auxiliary** verb? _____

d) Is it easy to determine the verb tense of the sentences above? Why? Talk about it with your classmates.

2 **Observe the underlined word in each sentence and choose its best description.**

a) I read the cook book <u>yesterday</u>.
- ○ finished action
- ○ action going on

b) She has never dyed her hair <u>before</u>.
- ○ determined time
- ○ undetermined time

c) <u>Last year</u> my grandpa traveled to France!
- ○ determined time
- ○ undetermined time

d) The exotic dinner hasn't started <u>yet</u>.
- ○ determined time
- ○ undetermined time

3 **Read and answer.**

> • I have played the piano since 2010.
> • I have already traveled to Australia.
> • I haven't cooked pasta this week.

a) What does the adverb "since" mean in the first sentence?

_____

b) Why does the second sentence use the adverb "already"?

_____

43

c) Why is the present perfect used in the third sentence?

_____

_____

_____

(4) Unscramble the words and form sentences with the present perfect.

a) her – car – already – Susan – wash.

_____

b) work – Brad and Carol – together.

_____

c) Canada – travel – to – already – Tammy.

_____

> **LANGUAGE PIECE**
>
> **Present Perfect**
> **Affirmative form:**
> Subject pronoun + **auxiliary verb** +
> (present tense **have/has**)
> + **main verb** + complement
> (past participle)

(5) Using the prompts, write sentences in the negative form of the present perfect.

a) I – pack – my bags – for the trip.

_____

_____

b) Betty – call – the pizza delivery place.

_____

_____

c) My friends – arrive – for my birthday – party.

_____

_____

> **LANGUAGE PIECE**
>
> **Present Perfect –
> Regular verbs**
> **Negative form:**
> Subject pronoun + **auxiliary verb** +
> (present tense **have/has**)
> + not + **main verb** + complement
> (past participle)

(6) Fill in the blanks with the present perfect negative form of the verbs.

a) The Johnsons _____ prepared for the winter. (to prepare)

b) Ronnie _____ studied for her final exam. (to study)

c) My classmate _____ passed his math test. (to pass)

44

7 Choose the best option to complete the sentences.

a) Why _____ so much rice today?

- ( ) has you cook
- ( ) have you cooked
- ( ) have you cooking

b) _____ they _____ the baking time for the cake?

- ( ) Have – checked
- ( ) Hasn't – checked
- ( ) Have – check

c) Where _____ you _____ soccer before?

- ( ) has – played
- ( ) have – played
- ( ) have – play

8 Read the answers and write the appropriate questions.

a) _____

Yes, I have finished my dinner.

b) _____

No, Daisy hasn't called me today.

c) _____

Yes, my teacher has talked about American history.

> **LANGUAGE PIECE**
>
> **Present Perfect –**
> **Regular verbs**
>
> **Interrogative form:**
>
> **Auxiliary verb** + subject pronoun +
> (present tense **have/has**)
> + **main verb** + complement
> (past participle)

9 Fill in the gaps with the present perfect form of the verbs.

a) A: _____ the new Marvel's movie?
(to watch)

B: Yes, I _____ it twice. (to watch)

b) A: _____ golf lately? (to play)

B: No, I _____ golf lately. (not to play)

c) A: _____ in a university before?
(to work)

B: Yes, _____. (short answer)

> TRACK 08
>
> **Vocabulary hint**
> "**Have not**" in the
> contracted for is "**haven't**":
> They **haven't** talked to the
> teacher.
>
> "**Has not**" in the contracted
> form is "**hasn't**":
> She hasn't talked to the
> teacher.

Let's listen n' speak

1 Listen and repeat the rhyme.

> Why have you waited for me?
> Because I have finished my tea.
> I have worked all day and I have planned to stay.
> But I'm tired so I have decided to go away.

a) Look back at the rhyme, underline the auxiliary verbs and circle the main verbs.

b) Rewrite the rhyme following the instructions.

- Change the personal pronouns **I** and **you** to the personal pronouns **he** and **she**.

_____
_____
_____
_____

- Change the verb tense from the affirmative into the negative form.

_____
_____
_____
_____

2 Work in pairs.

a) Prepare a short rhyme using the perfect tense.

_____
_____
_____
_____

b) Now, rehearse your rhyme and present it to your classmates.

Let's read n' write

1. Do you know any blog that tells people about different personal experiences and findings? Read a travel blog text about a paradisiac place and answer the questions about it.

Nomadic Matt

Ko lipe: the greatest month in all my travels

March 15, 2018/By Nomadic Matt

In November 2006, [...] **while** emailing my parents to let them know I was still OK, I saw a message in my inbox:

"Matt, I'm **stuck** in this placed called Ko Lipe. I'm not going to meet you as planned, but you should **come down** here. It's paradise! I've been here a week already. Find me on Sunset Beach. – Olivia"

[...]
I **looked up** Ko Lipe on a map. There was only a small mention of it in my **guidebook**. [...]

As I **looked around** the crowded Internet café and onto the busy street, it was clear that Phi Phi was not the tropical island paradise I had **envisioned**. [...] A quieter, calmer paradise held great appeal. [...]

Two days later, I took the **ferry** to **mainland**, a long bus to the **port city** of Pak Bara, and then the ferry to Ko Lipe. [...]

The ferry neared the island and came to a stop. There was no **dock** on Ko Lipe. [...]

As we walked to the other side of the island, I could see Olivia was right: Ko Lipe was paradise. It was all gorgeous **jungles**, deserted beaches, warm, crystal-clear blue water, and friendly **locals**. Electricity was only available for a few hours at night, there were few hotels or tourists, and the streets were simple dirt **paths**. Ko Lipe was the place I had dreamed of.

[...] I had no reason to leave. I was in paradise. [...]

My visa **ran** only until just before New Year's, so I would have to leave to renew it before **heading to** Ko Phangan for the holiday.

[...] I've never been back to Ko Lipe. [...]

GLOSSARY

Come down (to come down): encontrar-se com alguém em algum lugar.
Dock: doca.
Envisioned (to envision): imaginar.
Ferry: balsa.
Guidebook: guia.
Heading to (to head to): se direcionar / dirigir para.
Jungles: selvas.
Locals: (residentes) locais.
Looked around (to look around): olhar ao redor.
Looked up (to look up): procurar.
Mainland: continente.
Paths: caminhos, veredas.
Port city: cidade portuária.
Ran (to run): durar, ter validade.
Stuck: preso(a).
While: enquanto.

Nomadic Matt. *Ko Lipe: The Greatest Month In All My Travels*. Available at: <www.nomadicmatt.com/travel-blogs/ko-lipe-thailand-travel/>. Access: July 2018.

a) What was Matt doing when he got an email from Olivia?

- ( ) He was taking photos.
- ( ) He was drinking a cup of coffee.
- ( ) He was emailing his parents.

b) Where was Matt when he got Olivia's email?

- ( ) Ko Phangan.
- ( ) Phi Phi.
- ( ) Pak Bara.
- ( ) Ko Lipe.

c) Is Ko Lipe a famous place? What clues on the text support your answer?

_____

_____

_____

d) Why did Matt decide that Phi Phi was not the paradise he had imagined?

_____

_____

e) What was different about electricity in Ko Lipe?

_____

f) When would Matt have to leave Ko Lipe?

_____

g) Where would Matt go after leaving Ko Lipe?

- ( ) Ko Phangan.
- ( ) Pak Bara.
- ( ) Ko Lipe.

(2) Analyze the text and answer.

a) What are the characteristics of this text?

- ( ) Descriptive.
- ( ) Narrative.
- ( ) Persuasive.
- ( ) Informative.

b) What kind of information does it present?

- ( ) News.
- ( ) Cultural traditions.
- ( ) Historical facts.
- ( ) Personal experience.
- ( ) Specific locations.
- ( ) Travel tips.

c) Where can texts like this be found?

_____

d) What kind of language is used in it?

- ( ) Highly informal.   • ( ) Highly formal.   • ( ) Informal.   • ( ) Formal.

e) What text elements support your previous answer? Give examples.

_____

_____

f) What elements are part of this type of text?

- ( ) Address.
- ( ) Pictures.
- ( ) Subheadings.
- ( ) Graphics and numbers.
- ( ) Explanatory boxes.
- ( ) By-line.
- ( ) Title.
- ( ) Personal writing.
- ( ) Quotations.

(3) Thinking about blogs, check all that apply.

a) ( ) They are an online journal.

b) ( ) They are a paper printed journal.

c) ( ) They are for private entertainment.

d) ( ) They are for public entertainment.

e) ( ) They are meant to share personal opinions.

f) ( ) They are meant to share common sense rules.

g) ( ) They are meant to be about specific subjects.

h) ( ) They are meant to be about anything.

(4) How about creating a post for a travel blog? Follow the instructions.

a) Think about a topic related to your traveling experiences.

b) Take notes of all the relevant happenings.

c) Think about a title.

d) Write the text respecting the type of language usually used on blogs.

e) Exchange compositions with a partner and correct it, checking if it presents all the characteristics it should have.

f) Rewrite your article observing the corrections made.

g) Hand it in to your teacher.

CHAPTER 4
||| Tying in |||

National Geographic Kids

10 facts about indigenous aboriginal art and culture!

Explore Australia's rich Indigenous Aboriginal arts and culture with our 10 amazing facts…

Fact 1: The **Indigenous Aboriginal arts and cultures of Australia** are the oldest living cultures in the world! One of the reasons they have survived for so long is their ability to adapt to change.

Fact 2: The earliest Indigenous art was paintings or **engravings** on the walls of **rock shelters** and caves which is called rock art. **Red ochre** was being used for painting at least **30,000** years ago in central Australia.

Fact 3: One of the largest collections of Indigenous Aboriginal rock art is in the **heritage** listed **Dampier Archipelago in Western Australia**, where the rock engravings are thought to number in the millions.

Fact 4: Albert Namatjira is one of Australia's best-known Aboriginal artists, and the first Aboriginal painter to receive international recognition for his art.

Fact 5: Aboriginal people were in contact with the culture of other peoples, sharing ideas and skills, **long before** European occupation in 1778, including **Macassans, Melanesians, Dutch, Portuguese** navigators and **traders**.

Fact 6: At the time of European occupation, there were over **700** different Indigenous Aboriginal languages and dialects spoken in Australia. Now there are less than **250** still in use.

Fact 7: Land is fundamental to the **wellbeing** of Aboriginal people. The land is not just soil or rocks or minerals, but a whole environment that sustains and is sustained by people and culture.

Fact 8: One of the most **well known sacred sites** in Australia is **Uluru**, located in the centre of Australia. The first European explorers named it **Ayers Rock**. In 1985 the **Commonwealth** Government of Australia returned Uluru to its traditional owners, **Pitjantjatjara** and **Yankunytjatjara** people (also known as **Anangu**).

Fact 9: The **didgeridoo** is one of the world's oldest musical instruments and is made from limbs and tree trunks **hollowed out** by **termites**.

Fact 10: Aboriginal Arts and Culture can be found in some of the most incredible locations. **Lake Mungo** in **western** New South Wales is a site of great Aboriginal and archaeological importance, containing material dated to at least **33,000** years ago.

GLOSSARY

Commonwealth: comunidade política.
Engravings: gravuras.
Heritage: herança.
Long before: muito antes.
Red ochre: ocre, vermelho.
Rock shelters: abrigos rochosos.
Sacred sites: locais sagrados.
Termites: termitas.
Hallowed out (to hollow out): escavar.
Traders: comerciantes.
Wellbeing: bem-estar.
Well known: bem conhecido.
Western: ocidental.

National Geographic Kids. *10 facts about indigenous aboriginal art and culture!* Available at: <www.natgeokids.com/uk/discover/history/general-history/aboriginal-arts-and-culture/#!/register>. Access: July 2018.

Let's practice

1 What is "rock art"?

_____

_____

2 Who is Albert Namatjira and why is he important?

_____

_____

_____

_____

3 How many languages were spoken in Australia when the Europeans arrived? How many are spoken nowadays?

_____

_____

_____

4 Match the columns.

a) Largest collections of Indigenous Aboriginal rock art.

b) Best-known Aboriginal artist.

c) Languages before European occupation.

d) Land for Aboriginal people.

e) Well-known sacred site.

f) Oldest musical instrument.

g) Site of great archeological importance.

- Albert Namatjira.
- Whole environment that sustains and is sustained by people and culture.
- Dampier Archipelago.
- Didgeridoo.
- Lake Mungo.
- Over 700.
- Uluru.

EXPLORING

National Geographic Kids
- https://kids.nationalgeographic.com/world/

EXPLORING

- *Africa Is Not A Country*, by Margy Burns Knight, illustrated by Anne Sibley O'Brien. Millbrook Press, 2002.

PROJECT

Original Inhabitants

Organize yourselves into three groups and decide which group is going to research each of the following countries: Brazil, the USA, and Canada. The groups must research the original inhabitants of each country and focus on characteristics such as: language, food, music, and art. After gathering all the information, make a chart about those peoples and present it to the other groups.

UNIT 4
HAVE YOU EVER DONE VOLUNTEER WORK?

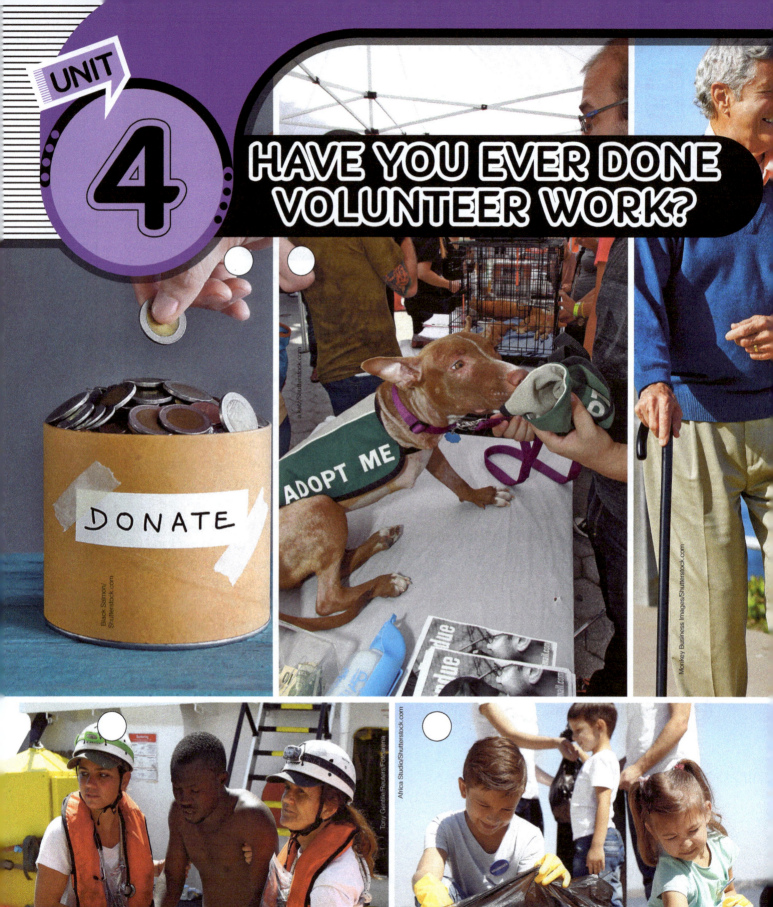

||| Get ready |||

1 What kind of volunteer work is it? Label the images accordingly.

a) Beach trash pickup
b) Doctors without borders
c) Elderly companion care
d) Money donations
e) Pet adoption fair
f) Serving meals

2 Have you ever done or heard about any of these activities? Mark the sentences T (true) or F (false) for you.

a) ◯ **Pick up** trash from natural places.
b) ◯ **Hear** about doctors without borders.
c) ◯ **Make** money donation.
d) ◯ **Visit** a pet adoption fair.
e) ◯ **Serve** meals in shelters.
f) ◯ **Be** a companion to an elderly person.

3 Write the past form of the verbs below and tell if they are R (regular) or I (irregular).

Family member	Past participle form	Regular/irregular
Pick up		
Hear		
Make		
Visit		
Serve		
Be		

53

CHAPTER 1

Let's practice

1) Match the words and their meanings.

campaign • charity • cooperation • donation • overcome

a) Help that you give someone; a situation in which people work together to achieve a result:
_____

b) A series of actions intended to produce a change in a situation:
_____

c) Money, food, clothes or any form of help given to people who are in a bad situation:
_____

d) Succeed in dealing with or controlling a problem:
_____

e) Kind acts that someone shows towards other people by helping them in different ways:
_____

2) Choose three words from the previous exercise and talk about your personal experience.

3) Analyze the following statements and answer the questions.

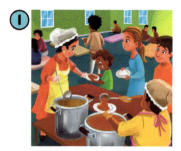

I) Jane has been a volunteer **for** fifty years.

II) Mathew has helped the Charity fair **for** four years.

III) Mathew has been a doctor of joy **since** he got in Med School.

IV) Jane has worked in the *Charity Donations Campaign* **since** 2018.

54

a) Do the sentences express the same idea regarding time/duration of the actions? Which are the words used to indicate time?

_____

b) Organize the sentences in the correct meaning category.

How long something has happened	
When something begun	

(4) **Choose the best alternative and fill the blanks.**

a) I have made donations for children's hospitals

_____ 2010. (for / since)

b) Leila has given people jobs _____ she founded a non-profit organization in 2008. (for / since)

c) Bon Jovi has had his charity restaurant

_____ 7 years now. (for / since)

d) Ronald's House has helped families _____ many years now. (for / since)

> **LANGUAGE PIECE**
>
> **Present Perfect – for/since**
>
> **For** – refers to a period of time up to the present: for twelve years; for two months; for a day...
>
> **Since** – refers to a specific time when something started in the past: since 2018; since she was a teenager...

(5) **Use the prompts to write sentences using the present perfect tense.**

a) I – live – London – 2 years.

_____

b) Jake – not have – a day off – three months.

_____

c) I – not eat – so much – Christmas.

_____

d) She – not see – her cell phone – yesterday.

_____

Let's listen n' speak

1 Listen to some stories about charitable celebrities and complete the text.

■ CHARITY

Meet four famously charitable celebrities

They are much more than good-looking actors.

Chris Hemsworth _____ a stand for the ecological crisis on how plastic negatively impacts our oceans since he was on Maldives in 2017.

"I _____ a large part of my life in and around the ocean. I want to inspire people to find a solution and protect the world's oceans".

Leonardo DiCaprio _____ a **long-time** climate activist for almost twenty years. He _____ **alongside** people **to raise** awareness in governments about climate change.

Angelina Jolie _____ a United Nations High Commissioner for Refugees (UNHCR) **Goodwill Ambassador** for more than fifteen years. She _____ in more than forty **field missions** in over thirty countries.

Keira Knightley _____ so moved by her eye-opening experience visiting a **refugee camp** in South Sudan in 2014, that she _____ the British public to support the 1.5 million victims of conflict there.

a) Discuss with a partner.

- Have you ever heard about these famous people's activism? Which one?
- Have you ever been inspired by a famous person? Who? Why?
- Have you ever thought about doing any charity or volunteer work? What?

GLOSSARY

Alongside: junto com.

Call on (to call on): recorrer, apelar.

Field mission: missão de campo.

Goodwill Ambassador: embaixador(a) da boa vontade.

Long-time: há muito tempo, antigo.

Refugee camp: campo de refugiados.

Take a stand (to take a stand): posicionar-se.

To raise: provocar, motivar.

LANGUAGE PIECE

Present Perfect – ever × never

Ever means at any time. Used in interrogative sentences.

Have you **ever** done...?

Never means at no time in the past or future, not ever.

I have **never** thought...

Let's practice

1 Look at the sentences and answer the questions.

> I have given the clothes I don't wear anymore to charity.

> Sam has set up a campaign to collect funds to the Children's Hospital.

> Taylor and Dave have overcome the expectations with their commitment to the environmental cause.

a) What is the verb tense used in these sentences? _____

b) Circle the main verbs in each sentence and write their base form. _____

c) What is different about these verbs? _____

2 Write the past participle form of the following verbs.

a) break _____   **c)** know _____   **e)** think _____

b) choose _____   **d)** take _____   **f)** wake _____

3 Complete the sentences with a suitable verb. Use the present perfect in the affirmative form.

> eat • know • write

a) I met Blair when we were in high school. We _____ each other for 10 years now.

b) Jake _____ many emails to his parents since he moved to the USA.

c) Jane and Mark _____ in that Japanese restaurant many times.

LANGUAGE PIECE

Present Perfect – Irregular verbs

Irregular verbs do not follow the rules to form the past participle form. Check the irregular verbs chart.

LANGUAGE PIECE

Present Perfect – Irregular verbs

Affirmative form:

Subject pronoun + **auxiliary verb** + **main verb** + complement
(present tense **have**/**has**) (past participle)

Negative form:

Subject pronoun + **auxiliary verb** + not + **main verb** + complement
(present tense **have**/**has**)   (past participle)

57

4 Write questions for the given answers.

a) _____

No, he hasn't written his final essay.

b) _____

Yes, I have already eaten breakfast.

c) _____

Yes, Margaret has read the email.

d) _____

No, they haven't spoken to the teacher about the test.

> **Vocabulary hint**
> **Word Stress**
> <u>cha</u>rity do<u>na</u>tion volun<u>teer</u>
>
> TRACK 11

LANGUAGE PIECE

Present Perfect – Irregular verbs
Interrogative form:
Auxiliary verb + subject pronoun + **main verb** + complement
(present tense **have/has**)   (past participle)

5 Choose an adverb that suits each sentence.
a) Why haven't you set up the campaign

_____? (already / yet / just)

b) I have _____ written an article about the bad impact plastic has on oceans. (already / yet / just)

c) Denise has _____ done a huge donation to the refugees fund. (already / yet / just)

LANGUAGE PIECE

Adverbs – never / ever / already / yet

Just means 'a short time ago'. (Affirmative sentences).

Already means something has happened sooner than it was imagined or planned. (Affirmative or interrogative sentences).

Yet means 'at any time up to now'; it suggests something is expected to happen. (Interrogative or negative sentences).

6 Rewrite the sentences using the adverbs in the correct place.

a) It's almost time and the volunteers haven't arrived. (yet)

_____

b) Have Peter and Marcus set up the beach cleaning campaign? (already)

_____

c) I have seen Martha catering for the homeless people. (just)

_____

_____

7 Let's play a board game! Flip a coin to move on the board.

HEADS = move 2 spaces **TAILS** = move 1 space

Let's listen n' speak

TRACK 12

1 **Listen to Amy and Mark's chat and answer the questions.**

a) What is the radio commercial about?

_____

b) What kind of work do they do? What kind of events and programs do they have?

_____

c) Has Mark already done any volunteer work?

_____

d) What kind of volunteer work has Amy already done?

- ( ) Elderly Homes.
- ( ) Food Banks.
- ( ) Park cleaning.
- ( ) Animals protection.
- ( ) Fundraising.
- ( ) Pet rescuing.

e) What will Amy and Mark probably do?

_____

2 **Imagine you have just heard the same commercial on the radio and you are talking to Amy.**

a) What would you say to her?

_____

_____

b) Now, compare answers with your classmates. Do you have similar ideas?

_____

3 **Working in small groups, look for the Petsmart Charities website and discuss the following topics.**

- What kinds of activities do they do?
- Would you like to help them?
- How could you help them?

Let's read n' write

1 **Discuss with your classmates.**

a) Have you ever seen or joined a charity campaign?

b) What kinds of causes can be targeted in charity campaigns?

c) What kinds of media can be used in charity campaigns?

d) What kinds of media usually call your attention?

2 Let's analyze the Water Aid campaigns' ads.

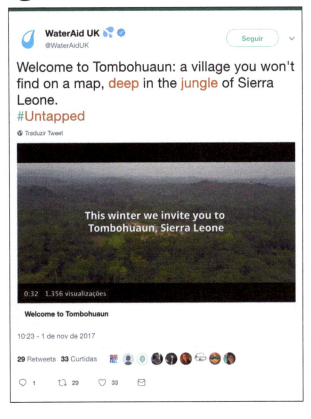

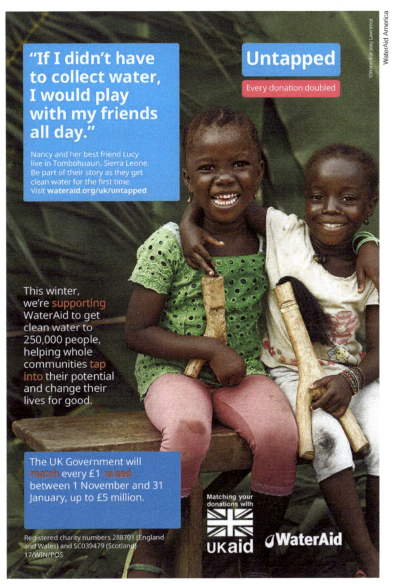

GLOSSARY

Deep: profundo(a), fundo(a).
Jungle: selva.
Match (to match): igualar, combinar.
Raised (to raise): levantar, aumentar, elevar.
Supporting (to support): apoiar.
Tap into (to tap into): acessar.
Untapped: inexplorado(a).

61

a) What is the name of the village? Where is it located?

_____

b) What natural resource is untapped there?

_____

c) What is this village's surrounding area like?

_____

d) What kind of activity do the children from the village do that is not supposedly done by kids?

_____

e) What is the aim of this campaign?

_____

_____

f) How many people will WaterAid campaign help?

_____

_____

g) What will the UK Government do?

_____

_____

(3) Think about the campaign ads and their characteristics and answer the questions.

a) What kind of information do they show?

- ( ) Cultural traditions.
- ( ) Dates.
- ( ) Historical facts.

- ( ) Numbers and values.
- ( ) Social needs.
- ( ) Specific locations.

b) What kinds of texts are they?

- ( ) Ad.
- ( ) Descriptive.
- ( ) Informative.
- ( ) Narrative.

- ( ) News.
- ( ) Pamphlet.
- ( ) Persuasive.
- ( ) Report.

c) Where can texts like these be found?

_____

_____

d) What kinds of texts are they?

_____

e) Who is the audience of these texts?

_____

f) What is the purpose of the text?

_____

g) What kind of language is used in it?

- ( ) Highly informal.
- ( ) Highly formal.

- ( ) Informal.
- ( ) Formal.

h) What elements are part of this type of text?

- ( ) By-line.
- ( ) Pictures.
- ( ) Campaign logo/aim.
- ( ) Captions.
- ( ) Contact information.

- ( ) Explanatory boxes.
- ( ) Institution.
- ( ) Introductory paragraph.
- ( ) Questions and answers.
- ( ) Quotations.

(4) After studying the previous campaign ads, let's plan a charity campaign for your school. Follow the steps.

a) Brainstorm all the needs of the community at the school surroundings.

b) Vote and choose one of the needs to design a charity campaign.

c) Choose a name for the campaign.

d) Divide yourselves into four groups:

- Each group will design an ad for the campaign.
- Decide what elements and information the ad should have.
- List all the tasks to be done and decide who is going to be responsible for each of them.

e) Make a chart reproducing the final version of your ad and hand it in to your teacher.

63

CHAPTER 4

||| Citizenship moment |||

5 ADVANTAGES OF VOLUNTEERING

With over 1.5 million registered nonprofits in the U.S., there are a lot of opportunities to make a positive impact in your community! So why volunteer? Based on the 62 million Americans that do so each year, here are five advantages of volunteering.

Christiane S Messias

1. It benefits the community

Make a real impact while engaging and connecting with people in the community.

 95% of volunteers say they feel that they are making their community a better place.

2. You will feel happy

One of the results of this positive impact on the community is that people feel happy and fulfilled.

 94% of volunteers say that volunteering makes their mood better.

 96% of volunteers feel a greater sense of purpose.

3. It reduces stress levels

Volunteers also show higher levels of self-esteem and more valuable interpersonal relationship than non-volunteers.

 76% of people say that volunteering decreases their stress levels.

GLOSSARY

Benefits: vantagens.
Enriched (to enrich): enriquecido(a) (enriquecer).
Illness: doença.
Mood: humor.
Nonprofits: sem fins lucrativos.
Purpose: propósito.
Reported (to report): relatar.
Self-esteem: autoestima.
Skills: habilidades.
Sound: healthy.

4. It keeps you sound

Good Mood + Less Stress = Good Health

 76% of people physically healthier after volunteering.

Volunteering can help people with health conditions. About 1 in 4 volunteers say that it helps them control a chronic illness.

5. It improves professional skills

Volunteering can also develop skills needed to grow professionally! Among people who say that volunteering has improved their careers:

 87% reported that volunteering has enriched their people and teamwork.

 75% felt that it improved their organization skills.

Based on: *5 benefits of volunteering*. Available at: <https://infographicjournal.com/5-benefits-of-volunteering/>; *5 surprising benefits of volunteering*. Available at: <www.forbes.com/sites/nextavenue/2015/03/19/5-surprising-benefits-of-volunteering/#4c4ed9f4127b>. Access: Oct. 2018.

Let's practice

1) How many nonprofit organizations are registered in the USA? How many Americans are volunteers?

_____

_____

_____

2) Match to the correct information.

a) It's good for the community.
b) It makes you happy.
c) It reduces stress.
d) It keeps you healthy.
e) It develops professional skills.

- 75% feel like improving organization skills.
- 76% feel like feeling healthier.
- 76% feel like lowering stress levels.
- 94% feel like improving their mood.
- 95% feel like contributing for a better community.

3) How many volunteers say it helps them manage chronic illness?

_____

_____

_____

_____

4) What skills does volunteering develop?

_____

_____

_____

_____

EXPLORING

- *Pay it forward*, 2000.
- *The soloist*, 2009.

PROJECT

Our Community

Group work: You have designed some ads for a charity campaign on Chapter 3. Now, use these ads to plan a charity campaign in your school.

- What are the tangible aims of the campaign?
- How is it going to be achieved?
- Who is going to be involved?
- What are the tasks each one will be responsible for?

65

REVIEW

1) Write a sentence with each word from the box using the present perfect tense.

> campaign • charity • cooperation • donation • endowment • philanthropy

_____

_____

_____

_____

2) Put the verbs below under the correct category. Then write the past participle form of each verb.

> arrive • hear • know • laugh • make • play • take • talk • think • write

| Regular verbs || Irregular verbs ||
Base form	Past participle	Base form	Past participle

3) Use the prompts below and write affirmative sentences using the present perfect tense.

a) my friend – arrive – from the USA.

_____

b) Jack – take – rock climbing lessons.

_____

c) I – make – a tattoo.

_____

d) My family – talk – about our vacation plans.

_____

(4) **Now, rewrite the sentences from exercise 3 in the negative form.**

a) _____

b) _____

c) _____

d) _____

(5) **Answer the questions using the given information.**
a) How long have you lived in Canada? (3 years)

_____

b) How long has Jake been a teacher? (2015)

_____

c) How long have you studied English? (6 months)

_____

d) How long has your sister played golf? (a long time)

_____

(6) **Fill in the blanks using ever, never, just, already and yet.**

a) Have you _____ been sick?

b) Our pizza has _____ arrived. It's time to eat.

c) Have you finished your food? No, I haven't finished it _____.

d) I have _____ traveled abroad.

e) My sister has _____ packed her bags for our vacation.

DO NOT FORGET!

HAVE YOU EVER
baked – painted – gone rock climbing – tattooed your body – dyed your hair – traveled abroad

HAVE YOU EVER...?
Used to ask if someone has already done something in any period of this person's life before now.

PRESENT PERFECT

Things that happened in an **indefinite** past moment.

Have you ever helped someone?

- Campaign
- Charity
- Cooperation
- Donation
- Endowment
- Overcome a difficult situation
- Philanthropy
- Set up an NGO

SINCE: When something has begun.

FOR: How long something has happened.

AFFIRMATIVE:
"I have played the piano <u>since</u> 2010."

Subject + have / has + main verb (**past participle**) + complement

NEGATIVE:
"We haven't studied Italian <u>for</u> 2 years."

Subject + have / has + NOT + main verb (**past participle**) + complement

INTERROGATIVE:
"Has he already traveled to Boston?"

Have/has + subject + main verb (**past participle**) + complement ?

PAST PARTICIPLE

REGULAR VERBS
Arrive → arrived
Bump → bumped
Cook → cooked
Laugh → laughed
Spill → spilled
Talk → talked

IRREGULAR VERBS
Be → been / Do → done / Get → got/gotten / Have → had / Take → taken / Say → said / Know → known / Wake → woken

ADVERBS

EVER
Means at any time, on any account:

Hey, Carl, have you **ever** listened to Elvis Presley's first record?

NEVER
Means at no time in the past or future:

My friends and I have **never** gone rock climbing... it's too difficult!

YET
Means at any or no time up to now:

I have not studied for the test **yet**, what about you?

ALREADY
Something has happened sooner than it was planned:

Susan is only four and she has **already** learned how to read!

OVERCOMING CHALLENGES

(UniCEUB-DF – 2014)

> A rise in temperature in the semi-arid region of Brazil has left rivers dry and cattle dying of thirst. The search is on for initiatives to combat desertification.
>
> Guardian Professional

The underlined words in the passage represent the:

a) present continuous tense

b) present perfect tense

c) simple past tense

d) simple present tense

e) simple future tense

(Uece – 2012)

The verbs of the sentences

"In the first task, the children **sorted** the shapes by color."

"...since studies **have shown** that bilinguals..."

"Why **does** the tussle between two simultaneously active language systems **improve** these aspects of cognition?"

are respectively in the:

a) simple past, present perfect, simple present.

b) present perfect, simple past, past perfect.

c) simple present, present perfect, present perfect.

d) simple past, past perfect, past perfect.

UNIT 5
HAVE YOU HEARD ABOUT THESE PLACES?

Beijing National Stadium

Built
Place

Lost City of the Incas

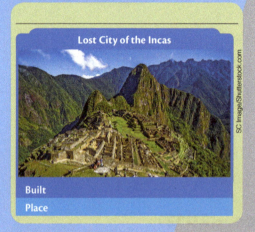

Built
Place

Flavian Amphitheatre

Built
Place

Walt Disney World

Built
Place

Cristo Redentor

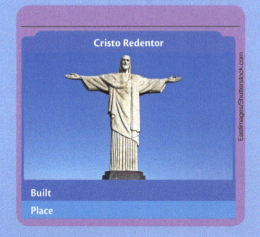

Built
Place

Sydney Opera House

Built
Place

||| Get ready |||

1 Can you guess it right? Use the information below to complete the information charts about these places.

Bird's Nest •	Beijing, China •	1450 A.D.
Christ the Redeemer •	Florida, EUA •	1931
Colosseum •	Cuzco, Peru •	1971
Disney World •	Rio de Janeiro, Brazil •	1973
Machu Picchu •	Rome, Italy •	2008
Nuns in a Scrum •	Sydney, Australia •	70-80 A.D.

2 Talk in groups.

a) Have you ever heard about these places? Have you ever been to any of them?

b) Which of these places would you like to visit? Why?

c) What is the most amazing place you have ever been to?

3 Do you know what landmarks are? Check all that apply.

a) ◯ Common.

b) ◯ Easily recognized.

c) ◯ Important.

d) ◯ Insignificant.

e) ◯ Modest.

f) ◯ National symbol.

g) ◯ Not recognizable.

h) ◯ Private symbol.

i) ◯ Stands out.

j) ◯ Unique.

k) ◯ Unknown.

l) ◯ Well-known.

4 Are there any landmarks in your country? Can you list them?

_____

_____

_____

CHAPTER 1

Let's practice

1 Read the text about **The Seven Ancient World Wonders** and answer the questions.

History

Seven Wonders of the Ancient World

Most of the original **ancient** wonders no longer exist. More than 2,000 years ago, many travelers wrote about incredible sights they had seen on their journeys. Over time, seven of those places made history as the "wonders of the ancient world". Today only the Pyramids of Giza still stand.

The Pyramids of Giza, Egypt
Built: About 2,600 b.C.
Massive tombs of Egyptian pharaohs, the pyramids are the only ancient wonders still standing today.

Hanging Gardens of Babylon, Iraq
Built: Date unknown
Legend has it that this garden paradise was planted on an artificial mountain, but many experts say it never really existed.

Temple of Artemis at Ephesus, Turkey

Built: Sixth century b.C.
This towering temple was built to honor Artemis, the Greek goddess of the hunt.

Statue of Zeus, Greece
Built: Fifth century b.C.
This 40-foot (12-meter) statue **depicted** the king of the Greek gods.

Mausoleum at Halicarnassus, Turkey
Build: Fourth century b.C.
This elaborate tomb was built for King Mausolus.

Colossus of Rhodes, Rhodes (an island in the Mediterranean Sea)
Built: Fourth century b.C.
A 110-foot (33.5-meter) statue honored the Greek sun god Helios.

Lighthouse of Alexandria, Egypt
Built: Third century b.C.
The world's first **lighthouse** used mirrors to reflect sunlight for miles out to sea..

GLOSSARY
Ancient: antigo(a).
Depicted (to depict): retratava (retratar).
Lighthouse: farol.
Wonders: maravilhas.

Elisabeth Deffner. National Geographic Kids. *Seven wonders of the ancient world*. Available at: <https://kids.nationalgeographic.com/explore/history/seven-wonders/#Pyramids-at-Giza.png>. Access: July 2018.

a) What kind of information does the text present?

_____

b) Do these wonders still exist?

_____

c) How old are these wonders? _____

d) Discuss with a partner:

- In your opinion, which of these Wonders is the most beautiful? Why?
- Would you like to visit The Pyramids of Giza in Egypt? Why (not)?
- If it were possible, which of the wonders that no longer exist would you visit?

② Do you know what period of time the following centuries correspond to?

a) Fifth century b.C.   • 600-501 b.C.

b) Fourth century b.C.   • 300-201 b.C.

c) Sixth century b.C.   • 400-301 b.C.

d) Third century b.C.   • 500-401 b.C.

③ These numbers are years. Can you write them in full?

a) 600 _____

d) 9,429 _____

b) 4,036 _____

e) 2,850 _____

c) 500 _____

f) 201 _____

④ Calculator spelling. Look at the numbers in full and write them in numerals. Follow the example.

a) nine hundred and eighteen _____

b) seven thousand seven hundred and thirty-eight _____

c) fifty-three thousand and forty-five _____

d) seven thousand seven hundred and thirty-four _____

e) three hundred and seventy-nine _____

f) five million, three hundred and eighteen thousand, eight hundred and four _____

LANGUAGE PIECE

Big numbers

Hundred	100	900
Thousand	1,000	9,000
Million	1,000,000	9,000,000

Let's listen n' speak

1 Pete and Jane are talking about time travel. Listen to them and answer the questions.

a) What did Pete invent? _____

b) Does Jane get excited about the invention? Why?
_____
_____

c) Jane also has a Time Machine. What is the difference between her invention and Pete's?
_____
_____

d) Where did Jane travel to?
_____

e) How many years did she travel into the past?
- ◯ 56,000,000   • ◯ 65,000,000   • ◯ 56,000   • ◯ 65,000

f) What did she see in the past?
_____

g) How many years did she travel into the future?
- ◯ 300   • ◯ 3,000   • ◯ 3,000,000

h) How long did she "stay" in the future?
_____

i) Did Pete believe that Jane traveled? Why?
_____
_____

2 Talk to your classmates.

a) Would you like to travel into the future or into the past? Do you think it is possible?

b) How far, into the past or the future, would you like to go? Why?

c) Have you ever seen a cartoon or a movie where people travel to the future? Which one? How did the travel happen?

Let's practice

1 Underline the verbs, rewrite them and label the sentences as **SP** (simple past) or **PP** (present perfect).

a) ( ) Lucy saw an ugly monument yesterday.

b) ( ) Have you ever been to Turkey?

c) ( ) We did not take food on the tour last week.

d) ( ) We have seen amazing ruins in Italy this month.

e) ( ) Mark has not eaten fast food for seven months.

f) ( ) Did you go on a boat tour in Sydney in 2010?

> **LANGUAGE PIECE**
>
> **Simple Past × Present Perfect**
>
> **Simple Past:** finished actions / happenings in the past.
> I saw four monuments **last** week.
>
> **Present Perfect:** unfinished actions / happenings that have a result in the present.
> I have seen four monuments **this** week.

2 Analyze the sentences and match them to their possible time markers.

a) We <u>have taken</u> great photos in Greece.

b) We <u>took</u> great photos in Greece.

- ( ) ago
- ( ) today
- ( ) 1998
- ( ) last Friday
- ( ) this week
- ( ) in January

3 Circle the mistakes and rewrite the sentences correctly.

a) Did Susan writes notes about our trip last year?

_____

b) Fred visit some museums in 2002.

_____

c) Our parents have make a photo album.

_____

d) Have Gonzales ever had a passport?

_____

e) The kids didn't ran in the art gallery yesterday.

_____

75

4 Complete the sentences using **ago** or **for**.

a) Yuri has lived in China _____ ten years.

b) The movie finished ten hours _____.

c) The museum closed fifty minutes _____.

d) Cara and Kieran have been married _____ five weeks.

e) Haram has studied Egyptian history _____ more than three decades.

5 Choose the best option to each sentence.

a) Marcia hasn't slept _____ more than 24 hours.
- ◯ for   - ◯ ago

b) The teacher rang the bell two minutes _____.
- ◯ for   - ◯ ago

c) Uncle Cleveland last visited us five months _____.
- ◯ for   - ◯ ago

d) Kevin and Martina have traveled to Hawaii _____ a fortnight.
- ◯ for   - ◯ ago

6 Look at the time markers and say if they refer to **HL** (how long) or **W** (when).

a) ◯ for seven years

b) ◯ a week ago

c) ◯ for ages

d) ◯ two years ago

e) ◯ for a few months

f) ◯ four hours ago

g) ◯ for five minutes

h) ◯ 20 years ago

i) ◯ for several hours

j) ◯ a few weeks ago

> **LANGUAGE PIECE**
>
> **Language piece**
> **Ago × For**
>
> **Ago:** how much time has passed since the action/event happened. (Simple Past).
>
> We got home **five hours ago**. (Five hours before now)
>
> **For:** the duration of an action/event up to the present moment. (Present Perfect).
>
> We have been home **for five hours**.

> TRACK 14
>
> **Vocabulary hint**
> **Notice the contractions**
> I have been ▶ I've been
> You have drunk ▶ You've drunk
> We have seen ▶ We've seen
> They have eaten ▶ They've eaten
> He has met ▶ He's met
> She has studied ▶ She's studied
> It has gone ▶ It's gone
> My friend has arrived ▶ My friend's arrived

7 Let's play a board game! Flip a coin to move on the board.

HEADS = move 2 spaces   TAILS = move 1 space

Let's listen n' speak

TRACK 15

1 **Listen to Moshe and Ella talking and say if it is T (true) or F (false).**

a) ( ) Moshe traveled to Africa alone.

b) ( ) Moshe has never been to Zimbabwe.

c) ( ) Star Wars was filmed five years ago.

d) ( ) Ella has not missed Moshe.

e) ( ) Ella has never seen Star Wars.

2 **Moshe and Ella are catching up after their summer vacation. Answer the questions about it.**

a) What countries did Ella visit?

_____

b) Who did Moshe travel with?

_____

c) Did Ella travel alone?

_____

d) When did Ella go to Africa?

_____

e) Has Moshe ever been to Africa? And to Tunisia?

_____

3 **Put the events in the order they happened.**

a) ( ) Moshe went to Africa.

b) ( ) Ella and Moshe hugged.

c) ( ) Ella watched Star Wars movie.

d) ( ) Ella went to Africa.

4 **Tell me more! Use the prompts from the box to find out about your friends' experiences and details about it.**

- to be to Pantanal
- to get lost from family
- to travel alone
- to miss a flight
- to send a text to the wrong person
- to lose your ID / passport
- to stay at a horrible hotel
- to get surprised

CHAPTER 3

Let's read n' write

1 Have you ever thought of traveling to India? Check this travel guide and answer some questions.

INDIA TRAVEL GUIDE

India presents one of the most unique sets of challenges of all. Its cultural diversity is cultivated by 29 states with different climates, **terrain**, and religions, besides its 122 languages.

60 DAYS — Visas and Flights

A valid passport and an Indian visa are required to enter and exit India. You can get the visa by applying at an Indian **embassy** (you cannot apply for a visa once you reach the country). Flights to India are quite long.

30 DAYS — Weather & Immunizations

The high season ranges from December to March and presents pleasant weather. From April to June, the weather becomes hotter and **monsoon** sweeps from south to north. Finally, from July to November, the monsoon **rain-showers** and heavy rain persists.

Indian government only requires immunizations for people coming from places with yellow fever registered cases.

- MIX
- HOT & DRY
- MONSOONAL
- COLD
- WARM & HUMID

7 DAYS — Packing

Make a list of all the items you should pack under clothing, personal care and medications, technological devices and documents.

0 DAYS — In India

IMMIGRATION AND CUSTOMS

Make sure you have a form for immigration, and one for customs.

TRANSPORTATION

India is known for having crowded cities and a chaotic traffic. **Stay on your toes**, the cheapest way of transportation are buses.

MONEY

Exchange your money currency for rupees (INR).

TIME DIFFERENCE

India has only one time zone, and doesn't observe daylight savings time.

CULTURAL FAUX PAS

- Refrain from using your left hand for any type of greeting or dining.
- Refrain from wearing shoes in religious establishment.
- Refrain from wearing shorts.

SAFE TRAVEL & NAMASTE!

GLOSSARY

Customs: alfândega.
Embassy: embaixada.
Monsoon: monção.
Rain-showers: pancadas de chuva.
Stay on your toes: fique atento.
Terrain: terreno.

Based on: India Travel Guide. Available at: <http://ecgroup-intl.com/wp-content/uploads/ITG-1.pdf >; Metric Conversions. Available at: <www.metric-conversions.org/pt-br/temperatura/fahrenheit-em-celsius.htm>; Lonely Planet. Available at: <www.lonelyplanet.com/india>; Centers for Diseas Control and Prevention. Available at: <wwwnc.cdc.gov/travel/destinations/traveler/none/india>; Trip Savvy. Available at: <www.tripsavvy.com/india-4138757>; Rough Guides. Available at: <https://www.roughguides.com/destinations/asia/india/>. Access in: July 2018.

a) What are the elements that make India a unique place?

_____

_____

b) Write **T** (true) or **F** (false).

- ( ) You can only get a visa at Immigration and Customs in India.
- ( ) The weather is better between December and March.
- ( ) There usually is monsoon, rain-showers and heavy rain between July and November.
- ( ) The Indian government requires a dozen different immunizations for all the people travelling to India.
- ( ) Packing is an easy task; you can do it on the day of your trip.
- ( ) When arriving in India, you only need an immigration form.
- ( ) Buses are the cheapest way to move around in India.
- ( ) You need to exchange your local currency into INR.
- ( ) India has more than one time zone.
- ( ) Do not wear shoes when entering sacred places.

c) How many different weather areas are there in India? What are they?

_____

_____

(2) Analyze the text and answer.

a) What are the characteristics of this text?

- ( ) Descriptive.
- ( ) Narrative.
- ( ) Persuasive
- ( ) Informative.

b) What kind of information does it present?

- ( ) Transportation system.
- ( ) Personal experience.
- ( ) Cultural aspects.
- ( ) Specific locations.
- ( ) Currency.

- ( ) Historical facts.
- ( ) Travel tips.
- ( ) Geographical information.
- ( ) Documents required.
- ( ) Health issues.

c) Where can texts like this be found?

_____

_____

d) What kind of language is used in it?

- ( ) Highly informal.
- ( ) Informal.
- ( ) Highly formal.
- ( ) Formal.

e) What text elements support your previous answer? Give examples.

_____

_____

f) What elements are part of this type of text?

- ( ) Address.
- ( ) Personal writing.
- ( ) Graphics and numbers.
- ( ) Subheadings.
- ( ) Title.
- ( ) By-line.
- ( ) Pictures.
- ( ) Quotations.
- ( ) Explanatory boxes.
- ( ) Introductory paragraph.

3 **After studying the previous travel guide, let's create our city's travel guide. Follow the steps.**

a) Brainstorm all the sections/topics a travel guide should present.

b) Organize yourselves into small groups to research each of the topics agreed upon.

c) Research official and trustworthy sources. .

d) Organize all the information gathered and translate it into English.

e) Each group writes a sketch of its travel guide section and exchanges it with the other groups.

f) Analyze the other groups' written texts and make suggestions and text corrections if needed.

g) Review your classmates observations and corrections made on your text.

h) Make a final version of your text and hand it in to your teacher.

i) After your teacher's correction, choose images to illustrate your section on the travel guide and write a final version of it.

j) At last, gather all the travel guide's sections and put them together making a complete version of your city's travel guide.

||| Citizenship moment |||

■ **CULTURE**

Guide to greeting people around the world
Here's how to greet people from different countries without any awkwardness.

By Suzy Strunter | Huffington Post | August 14, 2014

CULTURAL norms are confusing, but it's even worse when they're embarrassing: nobody wants to be that tourist who asks for cheese at dinner in Italy or forgets a gift in Japan.

We know how to "shush" people already, but before that, how do you greet someone in a new country? One kiss, two kisses, three kisses or none?

The rules change by region in certain countries, and they can vary between family, friends and new acquaintances – so be prepared for anything. But if you know the basics and pay attention to your surroundings, you'll be ready to adapt when your time comes for an introductory smooch.

Avoid that awkward head swivel with this simple guide.

Italy, Spain and much of Europe

Go for two quick cheek kisses: first on the right, then on the left. And if you don't know someone well, they may settle for a handshake. This is the standard for most places in Europe.

France

The bise (yes, it's notorious enough for a name) is complicated: Offer your right cheek as a starting point. The ensuing number of kisses will vary by region, anywhere from one kiss in certain areas to five kisses in huge swaths of the north. Just go with it. [...]

The Netherlands

The norm here is precisely three kisses, always performed right-left-right. Vague acquaintances won't kiss, and neither will two men.

Greece

Shake hands for acquaintances, but hug and kiss with someone closer. A two-cheek kiss is almost always accompanied by a back "clap," which can tend to come out more like a well-choreographed slap. [...]

Thailand

Press your palms together in a prayer pose, and bow your forehead to touch your fingertips. It's called the wai – the higher your hands are, the more respect you're showing.

GLOSSARY

A good ol' (a good and old): um bom e velho.
Acquaintances: conhecidos(as).
Back "clap": batida nas costas.
Bise: beijo (francês).
Bow (to bow): incline (inclinar).
Ensuing: resultante.
Forehead: testa.
Greet (to greet): cumprimenta (cumprimentar).
Handshake: aperto de mão.
Head swivel: giro de cabeça.
Issue: emitir.
Settle: decidir-se.
Slap: tapa.
Shush: silenciar.
Smooch: beijo.
Surroundings: arredores.
Swaths: carreiras.

India

People know to shake hands with Westerners, but if you're meeting a local and want to <u>issue</u> a typical greeting, place your palms together in prayer position, tip your head forward (but don't do a full bow), and say "Namaste". [...]

US

<u>A good ol'</u> handshake will do. [...]

News.com.au. Available at: <www.news.com.au/travel/travel-advice/guide-to-greeting-people-around-the-world/news-story/ca0f47df9244540b554259a08a5397b0>. Access: July 2018.

1 Discuss with your classmates.

a) How do you greet your friends and family every day?

b) If you travel or meet people from a different city, state or country, will you greet them the same way?

2 Match how close friends from these countries greet each other.

a) Spain.   **b)** Thailand.   **c)** France.   **d)** India.

PROJECT

Greeting etiquette

First discuss if there is any difference in the way people greet each other in Brazil and if they know any other type of greeting that is typical in other countries. Then, organize yourselves into small groups and choose a country to research its greeting etiquette. Once the research is done, present it to your classmates and act the greeting out!

EXPLORING

- *Junkyard Wonders*, by Patricia Polacco. Philomel Books.

EXPLORING

Countries and their Cultures
- www.everyculture.com

83

UNIT 6
HOW CAN THEY BE DESCRIBED?

||| Get ready |||

1 What do these images represent?

_____

2 How could these people be described? Write the following words under each image.

> adventurous • angry • calm • clumsy
> courageous • embarrassed • fun
> happy • helpful • honest • imaginative
> kind • nervous • persistent • relaxed
> satisfied • shocked • surprised
> thrilled • unhappy • worried

CHAPTER 1

Let's practice

1) Read the following profile and do what is asked.

People

Ray Charles Robinson, or just Ray Charles, was an Afro-American singer, **songwriter**, **musician** and **composer**. He was a very talented man, sometimes called "The Genius". He was very famous because he **combined** gospel, jazz, blues and Latin music.

At seven years old he had **glaucoma** and **lost sight**, becoming a blind man. He was a slim, medium figure with short black curly hair. He was a very sensitive and creative man.

a) Underline the adjectives used to describe appearance.

b) Circle the adjectives used to describe personality.

c) Who was Ray Charles?

_____

_____

d) Describe his looks.

_____

e) What were his personality traits?

_____

_____

GLOSSARY

Combined (to combine): combinou, misturou (combinar, misturar).

Composer: compositor(a).

Glaucoma: doença causada pela elevação da pressão intraocular, pode levar à cegueira.

Lost sight (to lose one's sight): perdeu a visão (perder a visão).

Musician: músico, musicista.

Songwriter: letrista.

LANGUAGE PIECE

Adjectives to describe character

See more information at **Language court**.

f) Pair up and complete the table.

My description of...	My friend's description of...
Myself	Me
My friend	Himself / herself

86

2 **Match the adjectives below to their correct descriptions.**

a) hesitant • ◯ Someone who is kind and has goodwill.

b) friendly • ◯ Someone who likes to keep things tidy and in order.

c) generous • ◯ Someone who is helpful, friendly and cares about others.

d) selfish • ◯ Someone who is not willing to work or make any effort.

e) respectful • ◯ Someone who shows respect to others.

f) easygoing • ◯ Someone who is willing to give money or help freely.

g) organized • ◯ Someone who thinks of his / her own advantage.

h) kind • ◯ Someone who is relaxed and not easily upset or worried.

i) lazy • ◯ Someone who moves or does things in a very awkward way.

j) clumsy • ◯ Someone who is slow to act because they feel uncertain.

3 **What is the opposite of...? Use the prefixes in, im, dis, un.**

a) honest _____ e) polite _____

b) reliable _____ f) kind _____

c) patient _____ g) happy _____

d) sensitive _____ h) loyal _____

4 **Complete the definitions below with suitable adjectives.**

a) Jane is the most _____ person I know! She's always smiling and being funny.

b) Peter is very _____. He never cheats in school tests.

c) Mary-Ann is a very _____ girl. She never believes things will be OK.

d) Chris' father is very _____. He has two jobs.

e) My sister is a very _____ person. Her room is always neat and clean.

f) Collin is always _____ to his classmates. He is always being bad to them.

g) Leslie is _____ because she has failed her math test.

Let's listen n' speak

1 Listen to Lucas and Pedro and answer.

a) What are they talking about?

- ◯ Physical characteristics.
- ◯ Personality traits.

b) Complete the chart with the personality characteristics you listened.

Pedro	Mariana	Julia

c) Who is not described in the listening?

- ◯ Pedro.
- ◯ Lucas.
- ◯ Mariana.
- ◯ Julia.

d) Where is the girl going tomorrow?
_____

e) What is she going to do there?
_____

f) What is it about?
_____

g) What time are the boys joining her?
_____

2 Put the images into the correct order.

88

CHAPTER 2

Let's practice

1 Read the sentences. Use **a** or **b** to connect the explanations to the examples.

a) The film is **boring**.

b) Teresa is **bored**.

- ◯ It is used to describe the feelings/how one feels.
- ◯ It is used to describe what causes the feelings.

> **LANGUAGE PIECE**
>
> **Adjective ending: -ed × -ing**
>
> **-ing:** cause.
> This film is boring.
>
> **-ed:** effect.
> I feel really bored.

2 Check the correct option to describe how they are feeling.

a)

Isobel is at home, on the sofa, reading.

- ◯ relaxed   ◯ scared

b)

Julian is about to start a test.

- ◯ surprised   ◯ worried

c)

Elijah arrived after a fifteen-hour flight.

- ◯ tired   ◯ interested

d)

I expected more from that interview.

- ◯ frightened   ◯ disappointed

3 Circle the correct option.

James: Man! This technology fair is really (fascinated / fascinating)!

Andrea: I happen to disagree. I'm (bored / boring).

Edith: Come on you two! Let's go and see the robots.

Andrea: Robots?

Edith: Yes, robots. There are some really (surprised / surprising) ones.

James: Nah… I'm not going to be (surprised / surprising). They are just pieces of metal.

Edith: Come on! I'm sure you'll find them just (amazed / amazing).

Andrea: I'm not sure if I'm going to be (amazed / amazing), but let's go!

89

(4) Complete the sentences with the correct form of the words in parentheses.

a) Do you think Nick will take one of your new kittens?

I don't know. He seemed _____ in them, though. (interest)

b) I heard you went to the rock concert yesterday.

Yes. It was really _____! (amuse)

c) I'm _____ that Monroe couldn't come to the party. (disappoint)

d) We were very _____ that you got a job promotion! (please)

e) Hank is buying a house. It's really _____ that he would buy it so soon. (surprise)

(5) Underline the wrong word in each sentence and write its correct form.

a) He is not interesting in the conversation. _____

b) He thinks the film was surprised. _____

c) This rainy weather is disappointed for him. _____

d) The pet enjoys playing but now he is tiring. _____

(6) Write a sentence with each of the following adjectives.

a) Amused _____

b) Frightening _____

c) Shocked _____

d) Annoying _____

(7) Pair up and interview your friend. Use the following questions.

TRACK 17

Vocabulary hint

-ed	-ing
bor**ed**	bor**ing**
interest**ed**	interest**ing**
amus**ed**	amus**ing**
annoy**ed**	annoy**ing**
excit**ed**	excit**ing**
frighten**ed**	frighten**ing**
shock**ed**	shock**ing**
satisfi**ed**	satisfy**ing**

- When was the last time you were terrified?
- Have you heard about any surprising news recently?
- What is the most thrilling thing you have ever done?
- What do you do when you are bored?

8 **Complete the sentences with a suitable relative pronoun.**

a) I've lost the bracelet _____ you gave me.

b) We know the musician _____ teacher was a famous pianist.

c) The children _____ come here are very poor.

d) The headmaster wants to know _____ locker was robbed.

e) The computer _____ they fixed is faulty again.

f) _____ is the man talking to the party hosts?

> ## LANGUAGE PIECE
>
> **Relative pronouns**
>
> **Who** – person / people.
> Pietra is the girl **who** is feeling embarrassed.
>
> **Which** – thing / things.
> I bought the books **which** are intriguing.
>
> **Whose** – possession, ownership.
> Bob has a daughter **whose** name is Leanne.

9 **Rewrite the sentences joining them by using the relative pronouns.**

a) I bought some comic books. They are fascinating.

_____

b) We're going to the show. The show starts at 8 p.m.

_____

c) They found a wallet. The owner is unknown.

_____

d) Wilma picked up the baby. He was frightened.

_____

e) You will meet the students. They are examples to others.

_____

f) The company used a great photo. The photographer remains unidentified.

_____

10 **Write sentences with who, which, and whose.**

_____

_____

Let's listen n' speak

1 Listen to Tonia and Margalit. What is the big event they are talking about?

_____

_____

2 What is wrong in the sentences? Rewrite them correctly.

a) Today is a special day for Tonia.

_____

b) Both girls are confused.

_____

c) Margalit is embarrassed.

_____

d) Tonia had a boring idea.

_____

3 Listen to Tonia and Margalit again and complete the gaps.

a) Tonia and Margalit _____ on the street.

b) Today is Margalit's _____ because she turned _____.

c) Tonia _____ get a present for Margalit, so she feels _____.

d) In the end, Tonia had a _____ idea and they decided to go _____.

4 Who said that? **T** (Tonia) or **M** (Margalit)?

a) ( ) I've had a very exciting day.

b) ( ) How are things?

c) ( ) Remember, I'm Jewish.

d) ( ) That's a little disappointing, but I'll live.

e) ( ) Why don't we go shopping now?

f) ( ) What an enchanting idea!

g) ( ) I'm a little confused.

92

CHAPTER 3

Let's read n' write

1 Discuss with your classmates.

a) Have you ever played a game in which you had to build up a character?

b) What kinds of characteristics can be used to describe a character/person?

2 Take a look at this game profile set up.

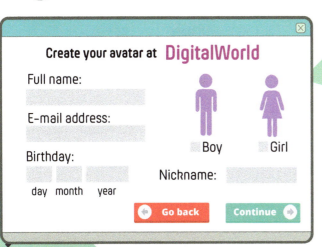

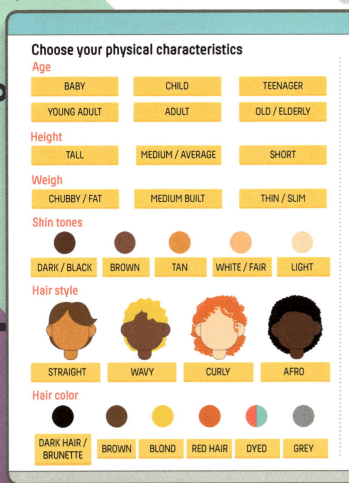

93

a) What kind of personal information does it request?

_____

b) What kinds of characteristics are required to build up the avatar?

_____

c) Label the groups correctly.

• _____	• _____	• _____
• brunette	• hazel	• baby
• blond	• brown	• young adult
• dyed	• green	• elderly
• _____	• _____	• _____
• straight	• braces	• tall
• curly	• scar	• average
• afro	• wrinkles	• short
• _____	• _____	• _____
• long	• brown	• chubby
• bald	• tan	• medium
• short	• fair	• slim

3 **Write the opposite for these adjectives.**

a) sad _____

d) lazy _____

b) dishonest _____

e) untidy _____

c) optimistic _____

f) polite _____

4 **Look at the images and describe the characters on your notebook.**

a)

b)

c)

Ilustrações: Marcos de Mello

94

5 Analyze the text and answer.

a) What is the main characteristic of this kind of text?

- ( ) Descriptive.
- ( ) Narrative.
- ( ) Persuasive.
- ( ) Informative.

b) What kind of information does it present?

- ( ) Physical characteristics.
- ( ) Cultural traditions.
- ( ) Personality traits.
- ( ) Historical facts.

c) What kind of language is used in it?

- ( ) Highly informal.
- ( ) Highly formal.
- ( ) Informal.
- ( ) Formal.

d) What text elements support your previous answer?

_____

_____

_____

e) What elements are part of this type of text?

- ( ) Graphics and numbers.
- ( ) List of adjectives.
- ( ) Pictures.
- ( ) Explanatory boxes.
- ( ) Subheadings.
- ( ) Quotations.
- ( ) Choosing boxes.
- ( ) Descriptions text.

6 What about creating your own avatar? Follow the instructions.

a) Go back to the text and select all the characteristics that your avatar will present.

b) Write down its description.

_____

_____

c) Use the box to represent it as a drawing.

d) Present it to your classmates.

CHAPTER 4

||| Tying in |||

■ BEHAVIOR

What is the Golden Rule?

[...] Do you like it when people are mean to you? Do you ever feel bad if you're left out of a game at recess? No one likes it when their feelings get hurt. But have you ever wondered whether your own actions make others feel the same way?

You may have learned from your parents that you should always treat others in the same way that you would like to be treated. That's called the Golden Rule.

It's also sometimes called the ethic of reciprocity. Reciprocity means acting in a way that's cooperative and benefits all who are involved.

The Golden Rule is sometimes stated in a negative way: don't treat others in a way that you would not like to be treated. Either way, the message is the same. If you want to be treated a certain way, then treat others that same way. If you don't want to be treated a certain way, then don't treat others that way.

For example, you and a friend are going to have pizza for dinner. Your mom bakes a delicious pizza and cuts it into eight equal slices. How should you divide the pizza?

If there are two of you, it means you should each get four slices. Of course, you can always choose to take five slices and leave three for your friend, if you're really hungry. But what about your friend? How would you feel if your friend did the same thing? If you'd like an equal amount of pizza, then the Golden Rule holds that you should only take half of the slices.

Really simple, right? If you think about it, though, it's obviously not as easy as it sounds. If everyone observed the Golden Rule, then there would be far fewer problems in the world today.

Although it's not always easy to live up to, the Golden Rule is widely considered to be a universal principle. That means that people believe it should be applied by all people in all situations, regardless of nation, culture, race or any other factor. This belief appears in some form across many religions and philosophies, and it has been included as a fundamental moral value of some governments and the basis for many laws.

[...]

Rather than merely abstaining from behaviors you yourself wouldn't like, take positive steps to help others in ways that we ourselves would like to be helped. In many places, it's part of being a good citizen and following the law.

Wonderopolis. *What Is the Golden Rule?* Available at: <http://wonderopolis.org/wonder/what-is-the-golden-rule/>. Access: July 2018.

GLOSSARY

Abstaining (to abstain): abstendo-se (abster-se).
Across: através de.
Amount: quantidade.
Bakes (to bake): assa (assar).
Benefits (to benefit): beneficia (beneficiar).
Cooperative: colaborativo(a).
Ethic: ética.
Fewer: menos.
Left out (to be left out): deixado de fora (ser deixado de fora).
Live up to (to live up to): agir de acordo com.
Mean: maldoso(a).
Merely: apenas.
Reciprocity: reciprocidade.
Slices: fatias.
Treat (to treat): tratar.
Wondered (to wonder): pensou (pensar, imaginar).

Let's practice

1. **Discuss with your classmates.**

   a) How do you feel when people let you choose / start something first?

   b) How do you feel when people don't share something with you or leave you aside?

2. **Choose the best alternative according to the text.**

   a) Which of these is not a way of stating the Golden Rule?

   - ○ Don't treat others in a way that you would not like to be treated.
   - ○ You should always treat others in a way that you would not like to be treated.

   b) Reciprocity means…

   - ○ acting in a way that benefits yourself only.
   - ○ acting in a way that's cooperative and benefits all who are involved.

3. **According to the text, why are there so many problems in the world nowadays?**

   _____

4. **In which society areas does the Golden Rule apply to?**

   _____

5. **Who should we treat with consideration and respect?**

   _____

6. **Why should we treat others well?**

   _____

7. **How do we determine how to treat others?**

   _____

PROJECT

Try it out

Are you ready to practice the Golden Rule? Discuss the following with your classmates:

- Can you think of a time when you felt left out or excluded by the behavior of others?
- How do you wish you had been treated in those situations?
- Can you think of any times when others might have been hurt by your actions?
- What could you have done differently in those situations?

Discuss the idea of universal truths with friends and family members and together come up with a list of possible universal truths.

Thinking about the Golden Rule, come up with two lists: things to do and things not to do. Try to come up with a list of 10 things for each!

EXPLORING

Internet Encyclopedia of Philosophy

- www.iep.utm.edu/goldrule/ Mindful Schools
- www.youtube.com/watch?v=RVA2N6tX2cg

EXPLORING

- *Inside Out*, 2015.
- *Hidden Figures*, 2016.

REVIEW

1. Complete the sentences with a verb in the present perfect or simple past.

a) She _____ smoking two months ago. (stop)

b) She _____ for several months. (travel)

c) _____ you ever _____ to Florence? (be)

d) _____ you _____ that TV show last night? (watch)

e) They still live in that town. They _____ there for ages. (be)

f) A friend of mine _____ the lottery three years ago. (win)

g) When _____ you _____ your homework? (do)

2. Fill in the blanks with for or ago.

a) We came to this town six months _____.

b) Chris has been studying Chinese _____ three years.

c) Our math teacher bought a big house three days _____.

d) I finished tidying my room half an hour _____.

e) Jackie has been playing the violin _____ only two months.

3. Complete the chart accordingly.

Base form	Simple past	Past participle
		been
buy		
get		
	had	
		known
meet		

a) Now, using the previous verbs, write true sentences for you on your notebook.

4 **Match the word with its definition.**

a) frightened • ( ) being afraid, very scared

b) tiring • ( ) helps to relax and calm down

c) surprising • ( ) being curious about something, wanting to know more

d) confused • ( ) that causes lack of interest, it is exhausting

e) irritating • ( ) that causes annoyance, irritation

f) interested • ( ) that has difficulty to understand

g) worried • ( ) being preoccupied

h) relaxing • ( ) that causes an emotional reaction, something that was not expected

5 **Choose the best option and complete the sentences.**

a) Dogs often feel _____ during fireworks.

• ( ) frightened • ( ) frightening

b) Satoru was _____ to hear about the earthquake.

• ( ) shocking • ( ) shocked

c) I think that rainy days in winter are _____.

• ( ) depressing • ( ) depressed

d) The meals at Immigrant's Cafe are _____ .

• ( ) satisfied • ( ) satisfying

6 **Circle the correct word.**

a) I don't understand this exercise. I'm very (confusing / confused). This exercise is really (confusing / confused).

b) My trip to the USA was cancelled. I'm very (disappointed / disappointing) because I really wanted to go. This situation is really (disappointed / disappointing).

c) The movie was so (exciting / excited). Let's watch it again, shall we? I'm very (exciting / excited) about it. I want to watch it again.

d) Kids often feel (frightening / frightened) when they see a horror movie. Horror movies are (frightening / frightened) for kids.

e) I do the same thing every day. My job is very (bored / boring). I'm getting (bored / boring).

DO NOT FORGET!

Famous places and LANDMARKS around the world:

Bird's Nest – Christ the Redeemer – Colosseum – Disney – Machu Picchu – Nuns in a Scrum

ADJECTIVES that can describe places

common – easily recognized – important – insignificant – modest – national symbol – not recognizable – private symbol – stands out – unique – unknown – ancient wonders – incredible – towering – well-known

PERIODS OF TIME AND TIME

A.D. → *ANNO DOMINI* (In the year of Our Lord, years of Christian era)

B.C. → Before Christ

AGO → Before the present, earlier.

FOR → How long something has happened.

NUMBERS

100 – 900	→	hundreds
1,000 – 9,000	→	thousands
1,000,000 – 9,000,000	→	millions

DESCRIBING PEOPLE

embarrassed	adventurous
friendly	angry
happy	calm
nervous	clumsy
relaxed	courageous
satisfied	fun
shocked	helpful
surprised	honest
thrilled	imaginative
unhappy	kind
worried	persistent

RELATIVE PRONOUNS

WHO → Refers to people.

WHOSE → Belongs to someone.

THAT or **WHICH** → Refers to specific people or things, add information.

Adjectives ending in -ED or -ING

ED → Describes feelings or emotions, how you feel.
e.g.: CONFUSED

ING → Describes characteristics of people or things.
e.g.: CONFUSING

SIMPLE PAST or PRESENT PERFECT

SIMPLE PAST
Used to talk about situations that happened in a definite time in the past.
e.g: I visited John yesterday.

PRESENT PERFECT
Used to talk about situations that happened in an indefinite time in the past.
e.g.: I have been to Japan.

OVERCOMING CHALLENGES

(UNB – 2013)

Based on the cartoon above, choose the correct answer.
– The man's decision to take up woodworking happened at an indefinite time in the past.

◯ Right.
◯ Wrong.

UNIT 7
WHAT CAREER WOULD YOU CHOOSE?

Caitlin Snow

She works at S.T.A.R Labs at Central City taking care of the team's health. She is a
_____

Simon Morrison

He works at the legal system at Star City fighting the crime at court. He is a
_____

Kara Danvers

She works at CatCo at National City writing stories about the city for the magazine. She is a
_____

James Gordon

He works at the police station at Gotham City trying to keep the city safe and out of criminals. He is a _____

||| Get ready |||

1 Read these sitcom characters descriptions and complete them with their correct professions. Use the word bank to help you.

> actor • doctor • lawyer • scientist
> chef • engineer • pilot • singer
> dentist • journalist • police officer • teacher

2 Chat with your classmates.

a) Do you know anybody who has any of these professions? Who are they?

b) Do you know what these people do in their jobs?

c) Would you like to follow any of those careers? Why (not)?

Jemma Simmons

She works for S.H.I.E.L.D at its labs developing specialized equipment and compounds. She is a _____

Cisco Ramon

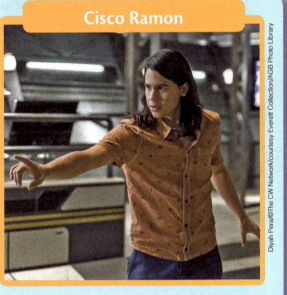

He works at S.T.A.R Labs at Central City developing machinery and devices. He is an _____

Chapter 1

Let's practice

1) Match the photos to the correct career descriptions.

a)
c)
e)
b)
d)
f)

- ( ) I work managing the kitchen of a restaurant, cooking special meals.
- ( ) I work cleaning up places and keeping things organized.
- ( ) I work judging cases at the court, applying the law.
- ( ) I work fixing cars and motorcycles.
- ( ) I work teaching kids at school and helping them at their academic life.
- ( ) I work flying big airplanes, traveling everywhere.

2) What is special about the following jobs? Match the profession to its special characteristic.

a) A cook
b) A model
c) A writer
d) A tourist guide
e) A dancer
f) A driver
g) A pilot

- ( ) has to know the route of a flight.
- ( ) has to have a driver's license.
- ( ) has to know all the elements of dance.
- ( ) has to know a lot of history.
- ( ) can work at home.
- ( ) has to be in good shape at all times.
- ( ) has to keep his/her hands clean at all times.

3) **Whose job do these things belong to?**

a)

Stethoscope.   Scalpel.   Mask.

_____

c)

Badge.   Hat.   Handcuffs.

_____

b)

Notebook and pen.   Microphone.   Camera.

_____

d)

Dryer.   Pair of scissors.   Comb.

_____

4) **Decode the words and find out the jobs.**

```
1 A  •  2 B  •  3 C  •  4 D  •  5 E  •  6 F  •  7 G  •  8 H  •  9 I
10 J  •  11 K  •  12 L  •  13 M  •  14 N  •  15 O  •  16 P  •  17 Q
18 R  •  19 S  •  20 T  •  21 U  •  22 V  •  23 W  •  24 X  •  25 Y  •  26 Z
```

a) 6-9-18-5-6-9-7-8-20-5-18 _____

b) 13-5-3-8-1-14-9-3 _____

c) 2-1-11-5-18 _____

d) 14-5-23-19-18-5-1-4-5-18 _____

e) 8-1-9-18-4-18-5-19-19-5-18

_____

5) **Put the words in the correct category.**

accountant • actor • architect • bank teller • doctor • lawyer
musician • nurse • salesclerk • secretary • singer • surgeon

Office work	Health related	Money related	Entertainment

Let's listen n' speak

1 Listen to the news about career choice influences and answer the questions.

a) What are the teenagers' role models?

- ◯ Media and popular culture.
- ◯ Parent's and family culture.

b) How many teenagers aged 14 and 15 say the media and pop culture influence their choices?

- ◯ $\frac{1}{2}$
- ◯ $\frac{1}{3}$
- ◯ $\frac{1}{4}$

c) What are these teenagers' inspirations to choose a job?

_____

d) What about graduates? How many of them are influenced by the media and pop culture?

_____

_____

2 Listen again and complete the table according to boys and girls professional preferences.

Career choices	Girls	Boys
1st		
2nd		
3rd		
4th		

3 Discuss with a partner.

- What kind of activities do you enjoy the most? How can they influence your career choice?
- If you could choose someone's job, whose would you take? Why?
- What may influence on the career choice?
- Who is your role model in terms of profession?
- Do you believe it is better to have a job in a big company, a small company, or work for yourself? What are the possible advantages and disadvantages of each?

Let's practice

1) Are these verbs followed by verbs in the gerund or the infinitive form? Place them into the correct column.

consider • continue • decide • dislike • don't mind
enjoy • have • promise • start • want

Gerund	Infinitive

2) Match the columns.

a) An accountant likes • ( ) to drive as carefully as possible.

b) A police officer avoids • ( ) to build safe buildings.

c) A driver tries • ( ) to work with numbers.

d) An engineer wants • ( ) to perform surgery or not.

e) A doctor decides • ( ) using a gun.

3) Unscramble the words to make correct sentences.

a) her / avoided / She / him / about / telling / plans

_____

_____

LANGUAGE PIECE

Infinitive × gerund

There are certain verbs that can only be followed by one or the other.

Take a look at the section **Language court** and find out more about it.

b) the / to / I / to / come / party / with / would / like / you

_____

c) having / enjoys / a / He / bath / in / evening / the

_____

107

d) during / kept / She / the / talking / film

_____

e) giving / hand / Do / mind / me / you / a?

_____

4 **Correct the sentences if necessary.**

a) I've finished to cook. It's time to eat! _____

b) He decided to study biology. _____

c) I dislike to wait. _____

d) I promise helping you tomorrow. _____

e) I can't stand to wake up early on the weekends. _____

5 **Complete the sentences with the correct form of the verbs in parentheses.**

a) I don't recommend _____ the bus at night. You might wait for a long time. (to take)

b) I hope _____ London next month. (to visit)

c) My sister suggested _____ to the museum in Toronto. (to go)

d) I don't want _____ home yet. The party is so much fun! (to go)

e) I enjoy _____ to pop music. (to listen)

f) The teacher promised _____ my essay today. (to read)

g) I've finished _____ the article for tomorrow's class. (to read)

h) Don't forget _____ the graduation pictures online, please. (to post)

6 **Answer the questions about your personal experiences and write complete sentences.**

a) Do you enjoy reading? _____

b) Do you mind waking up early on weekends? _____

c) Do you consider living abroad? _____

d) Would you like to learn to speak Spanish? _____

Vocabulary hint
Short _to_

I have _to_ go.

I'd like _to_ stay.

I want _to_ play.

7 Write sentences about yourself using the following verbs.

a) enjoy _____

b) try _____

c) hope _____

d) avoid _____

8 Tic-tac-toe. Pair up and follow the instructions.

Look at **Grid 1** and choose a verb, then write a sentence using it. Your partner will correct your sentence. If it is right, you mark the tic-tac-toe first; if it is wrong, your classmate marks it first. After that, your friend must make the sentence and you should correct it.

As soon as one of you wins a game, move to **Grid 2** and play again. Now the corrector will start the game.

Grid 1

love	hate	like
don't like	don't enjoy	enjoy
don't mind	would like	dislike

Grid 2

wouldn't like	dislike	think
like	enjoy	hate
don't enjoy	can't stand	love

9 Pair up and talk about how you feel regarding the following jobs.

bricklayer • carpenter • cook • dancer • doctor
dolphin trainer • engineer • lawyer • personal stylist
pilot • racer • store manager • taxi driver • teacher

A: I think writing a book must be nice.
B: I disagree. I think writing a book is boring./
I agree. I love creating stories.

109

Let's listen n' speak

TRACK 21

1 Listen to Amanda talking about her brother, Gustavo, and answer the questions about him.

a) What profession does Gustavo want to follow? _____

b) Why did he decide to look for a teacher?

_____

c) Besides writing, what else did he need to practice?

_____

d) What did he start to do every Friday?

_____

e) What are the results of his practice?

_____

2 Listen to the narration again. How many verbs followed by infinitives or gerunds can you hear? Write them down and then compare your answers with your classmates.

a) gerund _____

b) infinitive _____

3 Complete the chart about Amanda's brother.

Name	Dream career	Difficulties	Solutions	Results

4 Now, it is your turn. Think about a profession you would like to have and complete the following chart.

Name	Dream career	Difficulties	Solutions	Results

5 Pair up and talk about your dream career. Repeat it a few times, and, each time, tell what your previous partner told you about, plus your own answers.

CHAPTER 3

 Let's read n' write

1) What is the best way to find a job?

2) In your opinion: What are the easiest and the most difficult jobs in the world? Why?

3) What kinds of jobs are published on newspapers?

4) Look at this newspaper classifieds and answer the questions.

GLOSSARY

Aims: objetivos.

Chatty: pessoa que gosta de conversar (tagarela).

Eager: ansioso(a).

Figure: aparência.

Pleasant: agradável.

Skilled: especializado(a).

Tidy: arrumado(a).

To deliver: entregar.

To look after: cuidar de.

Vacancy: vaga.

APOEMA TRIBUNE

CLASSIFIED - VACANCIES JOBS

TRAINEE HAIRDRESSER
Full Time – 40 hours per week. Permanent vacancy. Work from Monday to Saturday. Responsibilities: welcoming clients, washing hair, serving coffee and tea to customers, and keep the salon clean and tidy. No experience is necessary. Apply Now!
andy@cut-above.servicesalon.com

MAGAZINE WRITER
Writers wanted! PEOPLE MAGAZINE is looking for writers for its website. Pay is based on the number of articles done. You may receive free tickets to events and free products to test. If you are chatty, interested, passionate, and skilled, contact us at info@peoplemagazine.com

CALLING ALL ACTORS AND ACTRESSES
Think you could be an actor? If so, we'd like to meet you! Working as an actor isn't easy but is very exciting and could be a great opportunity. Boys and girls should be over 21, have a pleasant figure and eager to learn acting skills.
info@brightactors.com

COFFEE SHOP MANAGER
Join world's number one coffee shop at CINNAMON COFFEE SHOP, where every café has the same aims: to create family-like teams and to give excellent customer service. Many different kinds of people come and work with us, so start your career at CINNAMON COFFEE SHOP today: choose the hours you work, get management experience, share your love of coffee. Join us as a team member. E-mail us at jobs@cinnamoncoffeshop.com

SUPPORT WORKER
Do you have the ability to care for others? Can you understand how older people feel? Are you a good communicator? Do you have good listening skills? Can you work on weekends? If you have answered YES to the questions above, we would like to hear from you. Pay $8.56/hour, free uniform, and excellent training. carreers@goldencare.com

BABYSITTER NEEDED
We need a babysitter to look after two boys aged 4 and 8 after school from 3 p.m. to 6 p.m., Mon–Friday. $40 a week.

HOLIDAY JOB
Do you want to earn some extra money this summer? Do you speak another language? We need French, Spanish or German speakers to work as a clerk for us in the City Museum shop. Tuesday–Saturday. Send CV to citymuseum@holidayjob.com

PART-TIME WORK
We are looking for breakfast and lunchtime staff to work in our restaurant as a waiter/waitress on Saturdays. Come in (9 a.m. - 5 p.m.) or call on 45618739.

NEWSPAPER ROUND
Looking for people to deliver newspapers on Mon, Wed, and Fri mornings. The paper round takes 50 minutes in the village of Cantaburry. Papers must be delivered before 8 a.m. Must have your own bicycle or motorcycle. Ask for more info at Cantaburry post office.

---

a) What ads mention payment rates?

_____

_____

b) Match the requirements to the correct job ad.

- actor
- holiday
- hairdresser
- newspapers deliver
- support worker
- writer

- no experience
- to be chatty
- to have pleasant figure
- to have good listening skills
- to speak another language
- to have your own vehicle

111

c) In which job would you have to...

- ... start before 8 a.m.?

- ... speak a foreign language?

- ... be passionate and skilled?

_____

_____

_____

- ... work on Saturdays?

- ... keep things tidy?

- ... be passionate about coffee?

_____

_____

_____

_____

_____

_____

(5) Match the words to the correct definitions.

career • chatty • trainee

a) A person who is being trained to do a job: _____.

b) Talkative: _____.

c) Person's chosen job and life's work: _____.

(6) What are the duties of these jobs?

Display items on a shelf. • Take care of elderly people. • Listen attentively.

Sell shop's items. • Serve food and drinks. • Wake up early.

Deliver newspapers. • Read stories and play with young children. • Wash hair.

Look after children. • Keep the place tidy. • Take customers' order.

Babysitter	Support worker

Paper person	Waiter / waitress

Hairdresser	Clerk

7 **Analyze the text and answer.**

a) What are the characteristics of this text?

- ( ) Descriptive.
- ( ) Narrative.
- ( ) Persuasive.
- ( ) Informative.

b) What kind of information does it present?

_____

_____

c) Where can texts like this be found?

_____

_____

d) What kind of language is used in it?

- ( ) Highly informal.
- ( ) Highly formal.
- ( ) Informal.
- ( ) Formal.

e) What elements are part of this type of text?

- ( ) Contact information.
- ( ) Graphics and numbers.
- ( ) Title.
- ( ) Pictures.
- ( ) Job descriptions.
- ( ) Employer's name.
- ( ) Subheadings.
- ( ) Job title.

8 **After studying the previous job ads, let's create our own classified. Follow the steps.**

a) Brainstorm all the jobs that you know.

b) Organize yourselves into small groups and decide on four jobs you're going to write about.

c) List all the requirements and activities that are part of these jobs.

d) Organize all the information gathered and create a job advertisement to each of the chosen jobs.

e) Exchange your ads with the other groups.

f) Analyze the other groups' written texts and make suggestions and text corrections, if needed.

g) Review your classmates observations and corrections made on your text.

h) Make a final version of your text and hand it in to your teacher.

113

Tying in

In some countries, it is common for parents to ask their children to do certain chores in exchange for an **allowance**, for example, doing the laundry, walking the dog or baby-sitting. This is a great way for parents to start giving their children more responsibilities, and encouraging them to find a job in the future and support themselves. Read the text below and **find out** why having a job is so important.

Education

Introduction to knowing it's important

So why is having a job and a career important? Well, here's our top five list:

Number 1

Here at The Youthhood, we say, "A good day is a pay day". In other words, if you have a job or a career, you can **earn** money. If you can earn money, you can buy things you need, pay your **bills**, have a place to live, and basically do things you want to do. Without money, you can't do much!

Number 2

Having a job or career makes you feel good. Yeah, you heard us right. Knowing you can do something well and earning money for your skills is a great feeling.

Number 3

When you work, you contribute to the community. You help make the economy and your community stronger. You are being a productive **citizen** (which communities like) and a valued community member.

Number 4

When you work, you **develop** new skills, learn new things, and create a record of employment. Then when you want to get a new or a better job, or maybe even go to college, your experiences can help you to do that.

Number 5

Last but not least, when you have a job or a career, you have self-respect, dignity, and **self-worth**. You are being responsible and making sure that you can take care of yourself. You are creating a solid foundation that you can **build on** to have a successful future.

Your first job may not be the type of job you have want forever, but it's a job that will give you skills you can use for a career that will last long after high school!

> **GLOSSARY**
>
> **Allowance:** mesada.
> **Bills:** contas.
> **Build on (to build on):** construir.
> **Citizen:** cidadão.
> **Develop (to develop):** desenvolve (desenvolver).
> **Earn (to earn):** ganhar.
> **Find out (to find out):** descubra (descobrir).
> **Self-worth:** autoestima.

YouthHood.org. *The Job Center – Knowing It's Important.* Available at: <www.youthhood.org/jobcenter/ki_index.asp>. Access: July 2018.

Let's practice

1 Read the text carefully and answer the following questions.

a) If you have a job, what can you do with your money?

_____
_____
_____
_____

EXPLORING

Project Britain
- http://projectbritain.com/teenagejobs.htm

Jovem Aprendiz
- https://jovemaprendizbr.com.br

b) Do you agree with item number 2 in the text? Why or why not?

_____
_____
_____

c) Once you have started working, what can you do next?

_____
_____
_____

PROJECT

My résumé

Have you ever thought about a job or career you would like to have? The first step to apply for a job is to write a résumé with your qualifications. Follow the instructions below and work on it.

- Personal Information (Name, address, birth date, age etc.).
- Skills (What are you good at? Math, languages, manual work…).
- Personal qualities (Are you an organized person? How about trustworthy and responsible?).
- Courses and certificates (What have you achieved so far? Do you take any courses like English courses, sports or arts?).

d) How can your job contribute to your community?

_____
_____
_____
_____
_____

UNIT 8
WHAT ABOUT YOUR HEALTH HABITS?

||| Get ready |||

1 Are those habits good or bad to our health? Place each image under the correct category.

Good habits				
Bad habits				

2 Discuss with your classmates.

a) Do you have healthy habits? Which ones?

b) In your opinion, what are the key habits to a healthy life?

c) How could you improve your habits to be healthier?

VII

VIII

CHAPTER 1

Let's practice

1 Have you ever heard about *Healthy Eating Plate*? Read the text and write T (true) or F (false).

NUTRITION

Healthy Eating: Plate & Pyramid

Created by nutrition experts to help people improve their eating habits, the Healthy Eating Plate and the Healthy Eating Pyramid are complementary to each other, respectively used as a guide for creating healthy and balanced meals, and as a guide for a **grocery** list.

It is important to understand that both healthy eating references present the importance of choosing healthier food items from each food group and that we must eat more items from some groups, like vegetables and fruits, and less items from other groups like **sweets** and fat.

To a healthier and more balanced life it is important to take care of our eating habits, as well as to be physically active every day, like running, playing, biking, and the like. Changes do not need to be done **overnight**. Take **one step at a time** and progressively change to a better and healthier life style.

GLOSSARY

Grocery: itens de mercearia.
One step at a time: um passo por vez.
Overnight: da noite para o dia.
Sweets: doces.

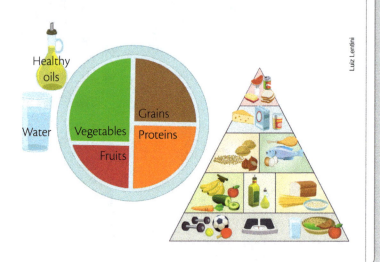

Luiz Lentini

Based on: Harvard T.H. Chan. *Healthy Eating Plate & Healthy Eating Pyramid*. Available at: <www.hsph.harvard.edu/nutritionsource/healthy-eating-plate/>; USDA – Food and Nutrition Service. *Team Nutrition*. Available at. <http://teamnutrition.usda.gov/resources/mpk_close.pdf>. Access: July 2018.

a) ◯ The Healthy Eating Plate can´t be used as a guide for a grocery list.

b) ◯ The Healthy Eating Plate can be used as guide for a balanced meal.

c) ◯ It is advisable to eat food item from groups like vegetable and fruits.

d) ◯ Physical activities are as importante as a balanced diet.

e) ◯ To a healthier life, it is not importante to take care o four eating habits.

2 Circle only the physical exercises mentioned in the text.

a)    c)    e)

b)    d)    f)

3 Match the food item to the correct food group.

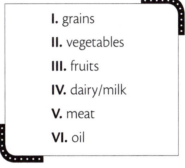

I. grains
II. vegetables
III. fruits
IV. dairy/milk
V. meat
VI. oil

a)
- peanut oil

c)
- oats

e)
- celery

b)
- curd

d)
- dragon fruit

f)
- shrimp

4 What's your favorite food? Give three examples of each food group.

Grains	Vegetables	Fruits	Dairy	Meat

Let's listen n' speak

1 Listen to a radio program giving some health habits tips. Mark all the tips you hear.

a) ◯ Be negative.
b) ◯ Do more exercises.
c) ◯ Drink less sweetened drinks.
d) ◯ Drink more sweetened drinks.
e) ◯ Eat breakfast.
f) ◯ Eat junk food.
g) ◯ Eat more fruits and vegetables.
h) ◯ Move less.
i) ◯ Have a short sleep.
j) ◯ Sleep more.

2 Based on the audio, discuss the following questions with your friends.

- Which of these recommendations do you follow?
- Who are the recommendations for?
- Do you agree with all of them? Why or why not?

3 What about applying the advice you listened to? Use the chart to mark the time you spend on your daily activities and keep track of your improvement.

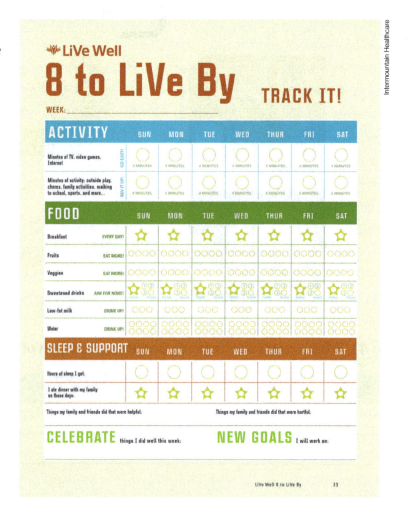

CHAPTER 2

Let's practice

1 Check the best reply for each statement.

a) I have a test early tomorrow morning.
- ◯ You should go to bed early.
- ◯ You can watch a movie to relax tonight.

b) I am trying to lose weight.
- ◯ You should eat healthy foods.
- ◯ You shouldn't eat more than twice a day.

c) I want to be healthy but I like sweets.
- ◯ You can drink soda.
- ◯ You should eat more fruits.

d) This milk doesn't smell good.
- ◯ You can't drink it.
- ◯ You shouldn't drink it.

2 Complete the dialogue gaps using **can** or **should**.

A: There is a lot to do in Toronto. For example, you _____ visit the CN Tower or the Aquarium or many other places.

B: Great, but what do you think I _____ do while I'm in Toronto?

A: It's not a good idea to drive in the city, the traffic is terrible and parking is expensive. You _____ use public transportation, it's very good.

B: _____ you tell me some fun things to do in the city?

A: In my opinion, you _____ visit the Royal Ontario Museum. It's amazing!

3 Use the words in parentheses to write sentences with **can**, **cannot** (**can't**), **should** or **shouldn't**.

a) It is raining today. (an umbrella / bring / you)

_____

b) I need to lose weight. (eat a lot of chocolate / you)

_____

c) I forgot to do my homework. (you / the teacher / tell)

_____

d) Mark is preparing a surprise party for his sister. (tell / you / her)

_____

LANGUAGE PIECE

Modal verbs: can and should

Can: indicates a possibility, an ability.

I **can** sing.

I **cannot** go to the movies today.

Should: indicates a suggestion, advice.

You **should** call your mother first.

He **shouldn't** miss so many classes.

4 Organize the words below under the correct category.

apple • calorie • carrot • drinks • exercises • habit
health • junk food • meat • milk • oil • water

Countable nouns	Uncountable nouns

LANGUAGE PIECE

Graded quantifiers

Graded quantifiers allow us to compare the quantities of two elements without specifying an exact amount of either of them. They always come before nouns and are divided into:

- **countable nouns:** many, (a) few, more, fewer, enough;
- **uncountable nouns:** much, (a) little, more, less, enough.

5 Now, place the quantifiers into the correct category.

enough • few • fewer • less
little • many • more • much

Countable nouns	Uncountable nouns

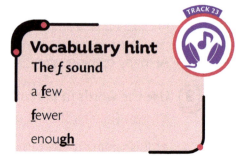

Vocabulary hint
The *f* sound
a **f**ew
fewer
enou**gh**

6 Circle the quantifier that correctly completes the sentences.

a) You can't eat so (many / much) calories a day.

b) We should all eat (fewer / less) junk food.

c) Most children don't eat (enough / much) vegetables every day.

7 Complete the sentences with the correct quantifier.

a) I know Mrs. Higgins has _____ good eating habits.

b) Children should drink _____ sweetened drinks.

Let's listen n' speak

1 **Listen to a nutritionist and her patient and answer the questions.**

a) What does a nutritionist do? _____

b) What are the best foods to eat? _____

c) What foods should the patient avoid? _____

d) Should the patient exercise? _____

e) How much sleep should the patient get? _____

f) Can the patient eat chocolate? _____

2 **Listen to the dialogue again and fill in the nutritionist's prescription for the patient.**

DD Form 1289
1 NOV 71
DOD PRESCRIPTION

FOR (Full name, address, & phone number) (If under 12, give age)
Marissa Domenico
Saint Claire Avenue, 239, Pittsburgh, PA, 15206, US.
717 – 555 – 0191

MEDICAL FACILITY	DATE
U.S.S.Pittsburgh Medical Center	*23 Nov 18*

1. *Eat enough of:* _____

2. *Avoid eating* _____

3. *Get* _____ *every day*

4. *Sleep* _____

EXP DATE: *12/20*

FILLED BY: *KMT*

R NUMBER 10072	*Wayne D. Jones* *LCDR, MC, USNR* SIGNATURE RANK AND DEGREE

MAY BE USED FOR
S/N 0120-LF-012-6201

Luiz Lentini

> **GLOSSARY**
>
> **Prescription:**
> prescrição escrita pelo médico ao pacientes para que eles sigam o tratamento indicado corretamente; receita.

3 Working with a partner, role-play an appointment with a nutritionist. Exchange roles.

> **Patient:** Think of your health habits and what you would like to improve. Ask the doctor for suggestions.
>
> **Doctor:** Listen to your patients, give suggestions on how to improve their health.

4 Look at this list of bad habits and think about the nutritionist's suggestions you have just heard. In groups, discuss the suggested topics.

> - Snacking non-stop even when you're not hungry.
> - Spending too much time on the couch watching TV.
> - Eating too much fast food.
> - Skipping breakfast.

a) Do you have these bad habits? Are there other bad habits you think you have?

b) How often do you practice them?

c) Would you like to change your bad habits?

d) How could you change these bad habits?

5 According to your discussion in the previous exercise, make sentences with some suggestions using the modal verbs **can** and **should**, and quantifiers you've learned in this unit.

_____

_____

_____

_____

6 Read the following proverbs about health and discuss their meanings.

> - An apple a day keeps the doctor away.
> - The beginning of health is sleep.
> - An imaginary problem is worse than a disease.
> - He who has no health has nothing.
> - Health is better than wealth.

124

Let's read n' write

1 Team up in small groups and discuss the following topics.

- Do you think it is important to have a balanced diet?
- What kinds of food are good for health?
- Do you check the nutrition information on food labels?
- Do you know what nutrition facts labels are for?

2 Take a look at the following food label and complete the activities.

I

Nutrition Facts
Serving Size 1 cup (228g)
Servings Per Container 12

Amount Per Serving
Calories 260   Calories from Fat 120

	% Daily Value
Total Fat 13g	20%
Saturated Fat 5g	25%
Trans Fat 2g	
Cholesterol 30mg	10%
Sodium 660mg	28%
Total Carbohydrate 31g	10%
Dietary Fiber 0g	0%
Sugars 5g	
Protein 5g	

Vitamin A 4%   •   Vitamin C 2%
Calcium 15%   •   Iron 4%

*Percent Daily Values are based on a 2,000 calorie diet. Your Daily Values may be higher or lower depending on your calorie needs:

	Calories:	2,000	2,500
Total Fat	Less than	65g	80g
Sat Fat	Less than	20g	25g
Cholesterol	Less than	300mg	300mg
Sodium	Less than	2,400mg	2,400mg
Total Carbohydrate		300g	375g
Dietary Fiber		25g	30g

Calories per gram:
Fat 9   •   Carbohydrate 4   •   Protein 4

https://www.fda.gov

GLOSSARY
Dietary: alimentar.
Serving: porção.

II

Nutrition Facts Serv. Size: 1 package, Amount Per Serving: **Calories** 45, Fat Cal. 10, **Total Fat** 1g (2% DV), Sat. Fat 0.5g (3% DV), *Trans* Fat 0.5g, **Cholest.** 0mg (0% DV), **Sodium** 50mg (2% DV), **Total Carb.** 8g (3% DV), Fiber 1g (4% DV), Sugars 4g, **Protein** 1g, Vitamin A (8% DV), Vitamin C (8% DV), Calcium (0% DV), Iron (2% DV). Percent Daily Values (DV) are based on a 2,000 calorie diet.

https://www.fda.gov

FDA. *Food Labeling Guide*. Available at: <www.fda.gov/downloads/Food/GuidanceRegulation/GuidanceDocumentsRegulatoryInformation/UCM265446.pdf>. Access: July 2018.

a) Which of the food items have:

	More	Less
Calories		
Sodium		
Protein		
Fiber		

b) What are the products serving sizes?

- I: _____
- II: _____

c) What do the following numbers refer to?

- 13: _____
- 45: _____

- 2: _____
- 4: _____

- 5: _____
- 8: _____

- 30: _____
- 0.5: _____

d) What vitamins are mentioned?

_____

e) What minerals are mentioned?

_____

f) What are daily values (DV) based on?

_____

g) How are daily values presented?

_____

(3) **Analyze the text and answer.**

a) What are the characteristics of these texts?

- ( ) Descriptive.
- ( ) Persuasive.

- ( ) Narrative.
- ( ) Informative.

b) What kind of information do they present?

_____

c) Where can texts like these be found?

_____

d) What kind of language is used in them?

- ( ) Informal.
- ( ) Formal.
- ( ) Technical.
- ( ) Non-technical.

4 Now it is your turn. After studying the previous nutrition facts labels, choose two industrialized foods that you eat regularly. Look for the nutritional information on their packages and complete the information in the chart. For each category write down which of the two options seems to be the best one.

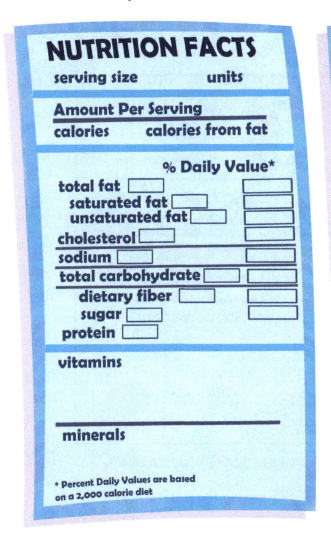

Marcos de Mello

||| Citizenship moment |||

GLOSSARY

Composting: compostagem.
Food-scrap: restos de alimento ou comida.
Overall: no geral.
Retail: varejo.
Stepping up (to step up): reforçando (reforçar).
Supply: suprimento.
Wholesome: saudável (comida).

Let's practice

1 Match the percentages to the correct information.

a) 31%   • Increase fruit and vegetable consumption.

b) 30%   • Reduce plate waste.

c) 70%   • Uneaten food supply.

2 What are the strategies mentioned on the infographic to reduce food waste at schools?

_____
_____
_____
_____
_____

3 What are the smart lunchroom strategies mentioned?

_____
_____
_____
_____
_____
_____
_____

PROJECT

Fighting food waste

Think about all the information on the infographic and team up to plan a school campaign to fight food waste. Research the food habits of your classmates from school and collect data on food waste. Once you have all information, plan a series of actions that can be done by your school mates to fight this problem.

▶︎ EXPLORING

Nutrition.gov
- www.nutrition.gov/smart-nutrition-101/myplate-resources

NHS Choices
- www.nhs.uk/Livewell/Goodfood/Pages/eatwell-plate.aspx

MyPlate Food Guide
- http://kidshealth.org/kid/stay_healthy/food/pyramid.html

ChooseMyPlate.gov
- www.choosemyplate.gov/food-groups

EXPLORING

Nourish Interactive
- www.nourishinteractive.com/kids/5-food-group-game

REVIEW

1 Which professionals use the following instruments? You will use words more than once.

a) Stethoscope: _____

b) Notebook and pen: _____

c) Mask: _____

d) Comb: _____

e) Scalpel: _____

f) Pair of scissors: _____

g) Handcuffs: _____

h) Hair dryer: _____

2 Choose the correct answer:

a) Would you like _____ with me to the party?
- ( ) to come
- ( ) coming
- ( ) to coming

b) Most people try _____ their money.
- ( ) to spend
- ( ) to spending
- ( ) spending

c) You shouldn't keep _____ so many chocolates.
- ( ) to eating
- ( ) to eat
- ( ) eating

d) I don't mind _____ early, so I offered to go tomorrow at 7 a.m.
- ( ) to work
- ( ) working
- ( ) to working

e) I miss _____ to my best friend since I moved to Canada.
- ( ) talking
- ( ) to talk
- ( ) to talking

f) My brother loves _____ pictures on social media.
- ( ) to posting
- ( ) posting
- ( ) to post

g) I still need _____ a lot in English.
- ( ) to learning
- ( ) learning
- ( ) to learn

h) Linda didn't like _____ her children alone but she had to go to work.
- ( ) to leave
- ( ) leaving
- ( ) to leaving

3 Place the food items into the correct category.

apple • banana • beef • broccoli • carrots • chicken • curds
lettuce • milk • oats • orange • popcorn • rice • shrimp • yogurt

Grains	Vegetables	Fruits	Dairy	Meat

4 Choose the more natural-sounding option.

a) Jane looks very sick. Maybe she _____ go to a doctor. (can / should)

b) You _____ smoke so much. It's a terrible habit. (can't / shouldn't)

c) Excuse me, miss. I'm lost. _____ you help me find the bus station? (should / can)

d) Mark has such a beautiful voice. He _____ be a professional singer! (can / should)

e) I know Rose speaks five languages, but _____ she speak Chinese? (can / should)

f) I _____ believe that you failed your driving test! (can't / shouldn't)

g) The plane tickets are too expensive. Unfortunately, I _____ afford them. (can't / shouldn't)

h) I know I _____ eat so much chocolate, but I absolutely love it! (can't / shouldn't)

5 Check the correct option.

a) sugar

• ◯ a few   • ◯ a little

b) time

• ◯ many   • ◯ much

c) houses

• ◯ less   • ◯ more

d) coffee

• ◯ enough   • ◯ many

e) cheese

• ◯ enough   • ◯ many

f) cars

• ◯ less   • ◯ fewer

g) money

• ◯ a few   • ◯ a little

h) calories

• ◯ much   • ◯ many

DO NOT FORGET!

JOBS AND PROFESSIONS

ENTERTAINMENT
actor – actress
singer – musician

OFFICE WORK
secretary – architect
lawyer – engineer

MONEY RELATED
accountant – bank teller – salesperson

HEALTH RELATED
chef – doctor
dentist – surgeon
nurse

ALSO IMPORTANT: teacher – pilot – police officer – scientist - nutritionist

HEALTHY HABITS

CAN
Ability, knowledge or permission to do something.

SHOULD
Suggestion, it is advisable that you do so, it is recommended.

You SHOULDN'T:
- Eat junk food.
- Drink sweetened drinks.
- Skip breakfast.
- Avoid exercising.
- Eat fats and sugar.

You SHOULD eat:
- Vegetables.
- Whole grains.
- Healthy protein.
- Fruits.
- Dairy.
- Grains.
- Healthy oil.

Hannah **can** speak French.

You **should** eat more fruits.

GERUND: base form with ING.
Use it after prepositions and after some verbs, such as *love*, *hate*, *like* and *enjoy*.

INFINITIVE: base form, with or without to.
Use it with MODAL VERBS, AUXILIARY VERBS and SIMPLE PRESENT.

EXAMPLES:
He thinks **about traveling** to the USA.
I **hate watching** horror movies.

EXAMPLES:
I **can teach** you how to ride a bike.
It is important **to listen** to the guide.

GRADED QUANTIFIERS

	QUANTIFIER	COMPARATIVE GRADE	SUPERLATIVE GRADE
COUNTABLE NOUNS	many / few	more / fewer	most / fewest
UNCOUNTABLE NOUNS	much / little	more / less	most / least

OVERCOMING CHALLENGES

(Centro Universitário de Brasília – 2012)

Choose the correct answer.

1 Susan is good _____ speeches.

a) ◯ at doing

b) ◯ in making

c) ◯ at making

d) ◯ in doing

e) ◯ on doing

2 " _____ what he's pointing at?"

"Sure I can. I'm looking at it."

a) ◯ Are you seeing

b) ◯ Can you see

c) ◯ Do you see

d) ◯ Where you seeing

e) ◯ Will you see

(UFF – 2008)

In the extracts below, the words with 'ing' are all verbs, except:

a) ◯ "humans are inflicting on other life-forms"

b) ◯ "this dysfunction is actually intensifying"

c) ◯ "sublime works of music, literature, painting, architecture and sculpture"

d) ◯ "the old way of being in the world"

e) ◯ "responding to this radical crisis"

WORKBOOK

||| Unit 1 |||

1. Complete the sentences using the correct form of say or tell.

a) His neighbor is crazy; she does not know what she is _____.

b) My mom _____ to shut up and concentrate.

c) Can you _____ me the time, please?

d) We have _____ the truth so my conscience is at peace.

2. Do you know these celebrations? Answer accordingly.

Holiday	Do people exchange gifts? If yes, which ones?	Is there any special food? If yes, which ones?	Is there a parade, party or ceremony?
Carnival			
Easter			
Festa Junina			
Christmas			

3. Check the correct form of the verbs to complete the sentences.

a) Who has _____ you where I live?
- ◯ said   • ◯ talked   • ◯ told   • ◯ spoken

b) Who were you _____ with on the telephone?
- ◯ telling   • ◯ speaking   • ◯ saying   • ◯ talking

c) Why did they not _____ thank you? That was so rude!
- ◯ say   • ◯ talked   • ◯ told   • ◯ spoke

4) Circle the mistake and rewrite the sentence correctly.

a) Julia said her would take a test the week after.

_____

b) Telma told Igor his mother have written a long letter.

_____

c) Philip said his mother were sick.

_____

d) The officers said the audience to be calm.

_____

5) Rewrite the sentences using Reported Speech.

a) Clara: "I often have some chicken with salad."

_____

b) Mike: "They live in Manaus."

_____

c) Danielle: "Susanna understands Japanese."

_____

d) Brian: "Leo is traveling to Australia."

_____

e) Susan: "Mike is working too much".

_____

6) Unscramble the words in one sentence by adding when, before or after.

a) Karen / monthly payment / she / got / her / paid her bills

_____

b) didn't tell / Maria / us / the party / will start

_____

c) Alice / going to work / the kids / brought / to school

_____

WORKBOOK

||| Unit 2 |||

1 Complete the sports' crossword.

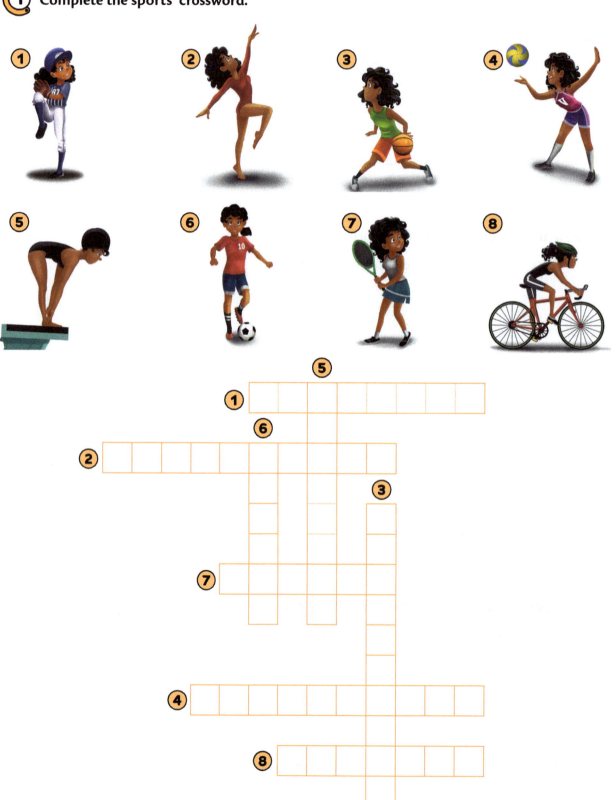

2 Complete the sentences with the correct comparative form.

a) He got up _____ she did. (early)

b) My iPad is _____ yours. (modern)

c) Lucia is _____ Philippa. (old)

d) Is this camera _____ than the other one? (expensive)

3 Complete the dialogues with the superlative forms.

a) A: What color did you paint the room?

B: I couldn't decide, so I painted it in _____ way possible. (colorful)

b) A: We all are bad liars.

B: I am sure I am _____ liar. (bad)

c) A: What movie are you watching?

B: Don't you know this? It's _____ movie ever made! (brilliant)

d) A: Did she like being a gymnast?

B: She sure did. Those days were _____ days of her life. (happy)

4 Observe the images and write suitable comparatives for them.

a)

_____

_____

b)

_____

_____

c)

_____

_____

WORKBOOK

||| Unit 3 |||

1 Match the columns.

a) paint   **b)** travel   **c)** rock   **d)** make   **e)** dye

• ( ) climbing   • ( ) a tattoo   • ( ) your hair   • ( ) a picture   • ( ) abroad

2 Complete the questions using the correct form of the verbs. Then answer with true information about you.

a) Have you ever _____ a picture? (to paint)

_____

b) Have you ever _____ abroad? (to travel)

_____

c) Have you ever rock _____? (to climb)

_____

d) Have you ever _____ your hair? (to dye)

_____

3 Complete the sentences with the correct form of the present perfect tense.

a) How long _____ in England? (he / to live)

b) Ricky _____ golf since 2016. (not / to play)

c) Amy _____ the same question three times today. (to ask)

d) I _____ all the episodes of my favorite TV series yet. (not / to watch)

4 Write questions using the present perfect tense.

a) She / visit / her grandma.   **c)** Maisy / wash / the dog.

_____   _____

b) Jeff / clean / the house.   **d)** You/ever/play/golf.

_____   _____

5 Unscramble the words to find out the base form of regular verbs.

a) clla _____

b) tosp _____

c) wathc _____

d) rorwbo _____

e) vairer _____

f) gulha _____

g) latk _____

h) coko _____

i) tesnil _____

j) cechk _____

k) nacel _____

l) kowr _____

m) vitnei _____

n) duyst _____

6 Use the given information to write sentences in the present perfect tense.

a) Affirmative: they – clean – the house

_____

b) Negative: she – close – the windows

_____

c) Interrogative: my sister – live – in Europe

_____

d) Negative: this package – arrive – from the USA

_____

e) Interrogative: Mark – listen – to music

_____

f) Affirmative: Ariela – invite – her cousins – party

_____

7 It's all about you. Write two affirmative and two negative sentences using the present perfect tense about yourself.

_____

_____

_____

139

WORKBOOK

||| Unit 4 |||

1 Find the following words in the word search.

campaign • cooperation • endowment • philanthropy
charity • donation • overcome • volunteer

C	A	M	P	A	I	G	N	T	P	E	E	O	Y	L
V	E	R	H	J	I	O	P	R	N	N	F	U	C	O
O	R	T	F	G	H	D	B	G	Y	D	T	Y	H	P
L	T	F	O	I	F	O	N	V	R	O	B	T	A	G
U	R	V	P	O	V	N	G	D	T	W	G	E	R	T
N	O	D	I	V	C	A	M	C	E	M	H	S	I	B
T	L	X	U	E	D	T	D	V	Q	E	Y	Q	T	E
E	T	S	Y	R	A	I	S	B	W	N	N	P	Y	W
E	E	C	T	C	S	O	A	R	R	T	M	O	R	S
R	W	L	E	O	Z	N	V	T	Y	R	J	F	Q	Z
L	E	D	R	M	X	D	C	L	T	D	R	T	W	A
C	O	O	P	E	R	A	T	I	O	N	T	G	D	Q
W	A	Ç	P	H	I	L	A	N	T	H	R	O	P	Y

2 Complete the chart below with the correct form of the verbs in the simple past and past participle tenses and write if they are regular or irregular verbs.

	Base form	Simple past	Past participle	Regular/Irregular
a)		Broke		
b)			Given	
c)	Borrow			
d)	Live			
e)		Ate		
f)			Read	
g)		Was/were		

140

3 Circle the correct option.

a) I have lived in Canada ———————————— three years. (since / for)

b) He has ———————————— left for school. (just / yet)

c) Frank hasn't arrived home ————————————. (yet / already)

d) We have worked together ———————————— 2015. (since / for)

e) Jane hasn't called me ———————————— three weeks. (since / for)

f) They've ———————————— played golf. (already / yet)

g) Our mother has ———————————— gone to bed. (just / yet)

4 Rewrite the sentences exchanging *since* and *for*. Look at the examples.

> I've lived in Canada **for** 3 years. (2016) ➜ I've lived in Canada **since** 2016.
>
> She's played golf **since** she was 5. (15 years old) ➜ She has played golf **for** 10 years.

a) He has dyed his hair **for** 10 years. (2009)

_____

b) They've lived in the USA **since** January. (3 months)

_____

c) We have talked **for** 3 hours. (7 o'clock)

_____

d) You have had that library book **since** Tuesday. (5 days)

_____

e) My mom has driven us to school every day **for** 3 days. (Monday)

_____

f) I have studied in the morning **since** February. (8 months)

_____

5 Prepare an introduction for yourself and write a short paragraph on your notebook. Make sure you use the present perfect tense.

WORKBOOK

||| Unit 5 |||

1 Write negative sentences with the simple past tense of the following verbs.

a) travel _____   **e)** look _____

b) buy _____   **f)** eat _____

c) visit _____   **g)** know _____

d) meet _____   **h)** borrow _____

2 Complete the gaps with the simple past tense of the verbs.

a) _____ you _____ fruits at the fair? (buy)

b) I _____ (write) an article and then I _____ it on Instagram. (publish)

c) He _____ (not go) to work last Monday. He _____ a headache. (have)

d) _____ you _____ your trip in the summer? (enjoy)

No, I _____ a horrible time. (have)

e) You _____ so funny yesterday. I _____ so hard! (be / laugh)

f) Janet _____ her best friend's birthday. (not - remember)

g) John _____ from his knee injury. (not - recover)

3 Use the present perfect tense to complete the sentences.

a) She _____ married for 12 years. (be)

b) He _____ Asia a few times. (tour)

c) They _____ alone. (never / travel)

d) The baby _____ sick since last week. (be)

e) Marcus and I _____ the stairs in The Eiffel Tower once this year. (go up)

f) Alissa _____ any piece of clothing since she lost her job. (not buy)

4 **Write the questions.**

a) _____

Yes, she wrote this letter.

b) _____

They have been to Japan twice this year.

c) _____

No, he has never tried reading during a car trip.

d) _____

We made that photo album in 2008.

5 **Circle the correct answers and complete the gaps.**

a) Dmitri has been in Europe _____ five years. (for / ago)

b) The train ride started twenty minutes _____. (for / ago)

c) They have worked here _____ 1999. (since / for)

d) I waited for you _____ forty-five minutes then I left. (since / for)

e) Heather finished packing a week _____. (for / ago)

6 **Use the prompts to write sentences with the most suitable verb tense.**

a) Negative - We - go - to the opera last Saturday

_____

b) Affirmative - I - never - hear - of this place before

_____

c) Interrogative - Vicky - win - a competition

_____

d) Affirmative -They - became - friends last year

_____

e) Interrogative - Your parents - meet - when they were at university

_____

f) Negative - Priscila - write a book

_____

143

WORKBOOK

||| Unit 6 |||

1 Decide if the sentences are C (correct) or I (incorrect). Rewrite the incorrect sentences making them right.

a) ( ) Whose tomb was discovered by Howard Carter and Lord Carnarvon in 1922?

_____

b) ( ) Whose is Batman's faithful companion?

_____

c) ( ) Who are the parents of your parents?

_____

d) ( ) Whose was the woman that had snakes instead of hair on her head?

_____

2 Answer the questions from exercise 1.

a) _____

b) _____

c) _____

d) _____

3 Write sentences to describe people in box A using the information given in box B. Look at the example.

A	B
<u>an air traffic</u> controller	is in charge of special services for guests at a hotel
a concierge	<u>controls the movement of aircraft</u>
a recreation worker	checks bags for contraband and documents at airports
a bellhop	carries guests' luggage in a hotel
a bartender	mixes and serves alcoholic drinks at a bar
a customs officer	creates and executes pastimes and diversions to bring relaxation

• An air traffic controller is a person who controls the movement of aircraft.

a) _____

_____

b) _____

_____

c) _____

_____

d) _____

_____

e) _____

_____

4 **Join the sentences by using a demonstrative pronoun.**

a) A woman has shouted. She was wearing a yellow dress.

_____

b) Some people ate all the candy. They were not very nice.

_____

c) Some homeless stopped our car. They looked needy.

_____

d) A boy broke the window. He got into trouble.

_____

5 **Give personal answers.**

a) Two things that make you frightened.

_____

b) A situation you consider surprising.

_____

c) Two hobbies you find interesting.

_____

d) Two events that made you worried.

_____

WORKBOOK

Unit 7

1 Read the clues and complete the crossword puzzle.

Across
3. A person responsible for the kitchen in a restaurant.
5. A person who designs buildings and supervises their construction.
6. A person who shows the way to tourists.
9. A person who takes care of people's teeth.
10. A person who defends people in a court of law.

Down
1. A person who works on movies and plays.
2. A person who writes books or articles.
4. A person who walks on the catwalk.
7. A person who plays a musical instrument in front of audiences.
8. A person who deals with customers in a bank.

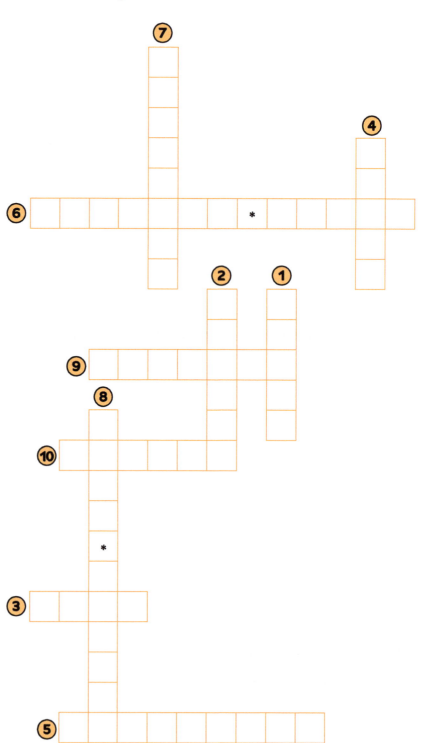

146

2 Decide if after these verbs we use **I** (infinitive), **G** (gerund) or **B** (both).

a) ◯ enjoy
b) ◯ have
c) ◯ need
d) ◯ don't mind
e) ◯ would like
f) ◯ keep

g) ◯ hope
h) ◯ begin
i) ◯ avoid
j) ◯ recommend
k) ◯ try
l) ◯ finish

m) ◯ afford
n) ◯ promise
o) ◯ can't stand
p) ◯ love
q) ◯ want
r) ◯ start

3 Complete the sentences with the correct form of the verb in parentheses.

a) I hope _____ from college next December. (to graduate)

b) The models wanted _____ on the catwalk. (to practice)

c) Charles dislikes _____ with a computer all day. (to work)

d) Sarah recommended _____ poutine while visiting Canada. (to eat)

e) My bicycle is broken. I need _____ it so I can ride it. (to fix)

f) After the accident, Jane never considered _____ a motorcycle again. (to ride)

4 Circle the mistakes and rewrite the sentences correctly.

a) A nurse enjoys to take care of patients.

_____

b) A journalist try getting all the facts accurately.

_____

c) I don't mind to wake up early.

_____

d) Children loves to playing in groups.

_____

e) My nutritionist recommended to exercise three times a week.

_____

WORKBOOK

||| Unit 8 |||

1 What is the food category?

dairy • fruits • grains • meat • sweets • vegetables

a)

_____

d)

_____

b)

_____

e)

_____

c)

_____

f)

_____

2 Are these habits G (good) or B (bad)?

a) ◯ Eating too much junk food.

b) ◯ Swimming twice a week.

c) ◯ Sleeping 8 to 10 hours a day.

d) ◯ Drinking soda.

e) ◯ Eating fruits and vegetables.

f) ◯ Using cellphones many hours a day.

g) ◯ Exercising.

h) ◯ Playing outdoors.

i) ◯ Drinking water.

j) ◯ Eating a lot of chocolate and sweets.

3 Complete the sentences with the appropriate form of can or should.

a) _____ you help me with my English homework, please?

b) You _____ exercise if you want to lose weight.

c) Paul is sick at home, so he _____ play football.

d) Drivers _____ drive over the speed limit. It's too dangerous.

4 Write the words into the correct category.

fruits • grains • milk • oats • oil • vegetables • water • yogurt

Countable nouns	Uncountable nouns

5 Organize the quantifiers into the correct category.

enough • few • fewer • less • little • many • more • much

Countable nouns	Uncountable nouns

6 Fill in the gaps with the appropriate quantifier.

a) How _____ pages do we have to read for tomorrow?

b) Mark drank _____ beer last night. He doesn't feel well today.

c) _____ people can speak ancient Tupi nowadays.

d) John had _____ money with him so he couldn't buy a movie ticket.

149

EXPERT'S POINT 11

WORLD RECORDS

20 best travel tips after 20 years of traveling

By Craig | January 15, 2018

1. Make Travel a Priority

If you want to travel more, you've got to make it a priority! [...]

2. Spend More Time in Fewer Places

When you're planning a trip, don't try to go everywhere and do everything – that's a recipe for burnout and blowing your budget! [...]

3. Don't Expect Things to Be Like They Are at Home [...]

4. Travel Does Not Have to Stop Once You Have Kids

[...] There are three key essentials to having a stress free family vacation. [...] Provide enough opportunities for them to rest and an environment to get a good night's sleep. [...] Choose a kid-friendly destination [...] and bring along a few home comforts. [...] Pack enough healthy snacks to keep them satisfied. [...]

5. Plan it Together

Sit down with all members of your family and talk about your trip. [...]

6. Talk to the Locals

[...] They usually have the best travel advice and insider knowledge on what to see, do and eat in their own town. It's truly amazing what you will learn by striking up a casual conversation. [...]

7. Learn the Basics of the Local Language

[...] Learning the basics of the local language is a great way to show respect and break down barriers. [...]

8. Travel In Your Own Backyard

[...] Start off by taking a day trip to a nearby town or a weekend getaway to the coast or mountains. Or simply explore your own town with new eyes. [...]

9. Do the FREE Stuff

If saving money when you travel is a focus for you, then one of our best budget travel tips is to seek out all the free things to do. [...]

10. Stay in Apartments or Airbnb (and share the costs) [...]

11. Fly Where the Deals Are

GLOSSARY

Blowing (to blow): estourando (estourar).

Break down (to break down): quebrar, romper.

Burnout: esgotamento, exaustão.

Get done (to get done): ser feito.

Getaway: fuga.

Go with the flow (to go with the flow) (slang): dance conforme a música (gíria), (dançar conforme a música).

Home comforts: utensílios do lar.

Looking for (to look for): procurando (procurar).

Once-in-a-lifetime-experiences: experiências únicas de vida.

Room: espaço.

Seek out (to seek out): procurar, buscar.

Start off (to start off): comece (começar).

Striking up (to strike up): puxando conversa (puxar conversa).

WORLD RECORDS

[...] Instead of choosing a destination and then spending days or weeks looking for a deal, considering flying to where the deals already are. [...]

12. Blow Your Budget

Every now and then, don't be afraid to blow your travel budget on those once-in-a-lifetime-experiences. [...]

13. Be Flexible

[...] leave room for flexibility in your itinerary. [...] Go with the flow a little and don't over plan. [...]

14. Don't Travel Without Travel Insurance

Probably our most important trip advice. [...] Especially if it's an overseas trip!

15. Working Holidays Are a Great Way to Experience the World

If you're interested in long term travel, consider a working holiday. [...] If you desire to live in another country and travel abroad, we recommend making it a working holiday! [...]

16. Pack Smart

[...] Our top travel packing tips are to select versatile, comfortable and loose fitting clothes and neutral colors that can be worn in multiple combinations so if something gets dirty you only have to change part of the outfit. [...]

17. Have More Than One Way to Access Your Money

[...] It's best to have more than one option. When we travel, especially overseas, we use a combination of: debit cards, credit cards, cash, travel money cards [...]

18. Use Credit Card Reward Points

[...] Get the best rewards credit card you can and use it to pay all your bills, groceries, fuel, eating out and earn reward points. [...]

19. Get Up Early

[...] When you get out of bed early it's amazing how much more you can get done in a day [...].

20. Put Down Your Phone and Camera

[...] If you spend your whole vacation looking at it through the confines of a lens, or keep jumping on Facebook every 5 minutes to see what everyone is up to at home, you are not fully present and can miss so much going on all around you! You've spent valuable money and time to be there in the first place, don't let the moment pass you by!

Ytravel. *20 best travel tips after 20 years of traveling*. Available at: <www.ytravelblog.com/20-best-travel-tips/>. Access: June 2018.

Expert's profile

Craig Makepeace

Craig Makepeace is the co-founder of the blog **yTravelBlog.com**. He has been traveling and living around the world since 2002 and has visited over 40 countries and lived in five.

PROJECT

Crazy Travel Mission

In small groups, choose the destination of your Crazy Travel Mission. Keep the following rules in mind:

- It can only be one place.
- Decide if your mission is either already finished or still happening.
- Follow your teacher's instructions to organize your poster. Collect all the needed information and use your imagination!

EXPERT'S POINT 11

■ **NEWS IN HEALTH**

Creating Healthy Habits

Make Better Choices Easier

We know that making healthy choices can help us feel better and live longer. Maybe you've already tried to eat better, get more exercise or sleep, [...] or reduce stress. It's not easy. But research shows how you can **boost** your ability to create and sustain a healthy lifestyle.

"It's frustrating to experience **setbacks** when you're trying to make healthy changes and **reach** a goal," says NIH **behavior** change expert Dr. Susan Czajkowski. "The good news is that decades of research show that change is possible, and there are proven strategies you can use to **set yourself up** for success."

Lots of things you do impact your health and quality of life, now and in the future. You can reduce your risk for the most common, costly, and preventable health problems [...] by making healthy choices.

Know Your Habits

[...]

"The first step to changing your behavior is to create an **awareness** around what you do regularly," explains Dr. Lisa Marsch, an expert in behavior change at Dartmouth College. "Look for **patterns** in your behavior and what **triggers** the unhealthy habits you want to change."

[...] "You can develop ways **to disrupt** those patterns and create new ones," Marsch says. [...]

Make a Plan

Make a plan that includes small, **reasonable** goals and specific actions you'll take to move toward them.

[...]

Consider what you think you'll need to be successful. How can you change things around you to support your goals? You might need **to stock up** on healthy foods, remove temptations, or find a special spot to relax.

[...]

It's also important to plan for obstacles. Think about what might **derail** your best efforts to live healthier. How can you still make healthy choices during unexpected situations, in stressful times, or when tempted by old habits?

Stay on Track

[...]

"Identify negative thoughts and turn them into realistic, productive ones," Marsch advises.

[...]

"The more you practice self-control, the better you become at it," says Dr. Leonard Epstein, who studies behavior change and decision-making at the University at Buffalo. "You develop the capacity to act and react another way."

Think About the Future

Epstein has found that some people have a harder time than others resisting their impulses. He calls this "delay discounting," where you discount, or **undervalue**, the larger benefits of waiting in favor of smaller immediate rewards. [...]

Focusing on how a change might heal your body and enhance your life can help. [...]

Be Patient

Sometimes when you're trying to adopt healthier habits, other health issues can get in the way.

[...]

You're never too **out of shape**, too **overweight**, or too old to make healthy changes. Try different strategies until you find what works best for you.

"Things may not go as planned, and that's okay," Czajkowski says. "Change is a process. What's most important is to keep moving forward."

National Institutes of Health. Department of Health and Human Services. News in Health. Creating Healthy Habits. Available at: <https://newsinhealth.nih.gov/2018/03/creating-healthy-habits>. Access: July 2018.

GLOSSARY

Awareness: consciência.
Behavior: comportamento.
Boost (to boost): impulsionar.
Derail (to derail): desencaminhar.
Out of shape: fora de forma.
Overweight: acima do peso, sobrepeso.
Patterns: padrões.
Reach (to reach): alcançar.
Reasonable: razoável.
Set yourself up (to set yourself up): preparar-se.
Setbacks: retrocessos.
To disrupt: romper.
To stock up: estocar.
Triggers (to trigger): desencadeia, provoca (desencadear, provocar).
Undervalue (to undervalue): subestima (subestimar).

PROJECT

Healthy Habits Poster

Using the information you have learned in this unit, design a poster that illustrates ways to keep healthy habits.

Your poster should include:

- specific healthy habits recommendations;
- two or three supporting facts about the recommendations;
- relevant diagrams or pictures;
- a list of sources showing where the information came from.

Each group has to be prepared to present/explain their posters to the class.

Expert's profile

NIH News in Health

The National Institutes of Health (NIH) is the North American medical research agency whose goal is to improve people's health and save lives through scientific discovery.
NIH News in Health is a monthly newsletter with practical health information and tips based on NIH research findings. NIH medical experts and NIH-supported scientists at universities and medical schools ensure accuracy by reviewing articles before publication. A new issue is published on the first Monday of each month.

FOCUS ON CULTURE 1

VOLUNTEERING

IT IS EASIER THAN YOU THINK!

RESEARCH!

Who would you like to help?

10 million NGOs

There are around 10 million NGOs around the world who need your help: you can support people, animals, the environment, and more. Before action, it is important to look for information!

ACT!

It is more rewarding than you think!

970 million volunteers

There are 970 million volunteers worldwide. In terms of economic impact for the planet, the value of volunteer work is US$ 1.348 trillion or 2.4 per cent of the entire global economy.

DONATE!
Donating is also caring!

31% of people have already donated money or goods for charity at some point of their lives. That means 2.1 billion people have already helped with money, clothes, food, and other.

The term "nongovernmental organization" (NGO) was created in Article 71 of the Charter of the United Nations Organization, in 1945. An NGO is a type of organization independent of government influence and not for profit. NGOs usually have social relevance and fight for helping people, causes, animals, places, and everything that needs to be helped.

Cristiane S. Messias

PROJECT

Work in groups and create a poster that you and your classmates can use to teach people about the importance of volunteering, donating and helping. Be creative: you may draw, cut and paste or even research information about any specific NGO or organization you would like to support.

Based on: *Global NGO Technology Report*. Available at: <http://techreport.ngo/>; *25 fatos e estatísticas sobre ONGs ao redor do mundo*. Available at: <www.terra.com.br/noticias/dino/25-fatos-e-estatisticas-sobre-ongs-ao-redor-do-mudo, 92e1d57491aa347c6f7d701f913a7ed75sklds7x.html>; *Charter of the United Nations*. Available at: <www.un.org/en/charter-united-nations/>. Access: July 2018.

155

FOCUS ON CULTURE II

HEALTHY EATING HABITS

Servings per day: 9

EAT ENERGETIC FOODS

The energetic food group is constituted by carbohydrates and greases: rice, pasta, sugars, and oils. This group gives us physical energy to do something.

EAT CONSTRUCTIVE FOODS

These foods are rich in protein. These substances allow the growth and the reproduction of our tissues. They are responsible for the formation of muscles, skin, hair, and other body parts. Beef, fish, eggs, milk, and all type of dairy are some of the constructive foods.

Servings per day: 9

Servings per day

7

EAT REGULATIVE FOODS

Food that provides the vitamins and nutrients needed for complementing energy and regulator, and for keeping the body functioning: fruits, vegetables, and water.

HEALTHY EATING PLATE

5% HEALTHY OILS
Fat, oil, sugar, and sweets.

45% Fruits and vegetables.

VEGETABLES
FRUITS
WHOLE GRAINS
HEALTHY PROTEIN

BEVERAGES
Water, tea, coffee, limited milk/dairy, and juice.

25% Bread, pasta, and cereals.

25% Meat, fish, milk, and eggs.

2 Liters per day — **DRINK WATER**

PROJECT

Pie Chart and Donation Campaign

Work in groups and discuss your own eating habits with your classmates. Make an eating plate that reflects your current eating habits and another one that reflects what you should eat in order to be healthier. Then, compare both of them with your classmates and with the suggested eating plate on the infographic.

Based on: American Society for Nutrition. Available at: <https://nutrition.org/>; Associação Brasileira de Nutrição - ASBRAN. Available at: <www.asbran.org.br/arquivos/PRONUTRI-SICNUT-VD.pdf>; The nutrition Source - Harvard T.H. Chan. Available at: <www.hsph.harvard.edu/nutritionsource/healthy-eating-plate/>. Access: July 2018.

LANGUAGE COURT

||| Unit 1 |||

Page 15

The verbs **to say**, **to tell**, **to talk**, and **to speak** are used to express different forms of verbal communication. Take a look:

Say	
Use	**Example**
To speak words to somebody. Used in direct and indirect speech.	She said that it was my last chance on the team. All that I said to you was true.

Talk	
Use	**Example**
To converse with another person about something. Usually refers to conversational exchanges and informal communication.	When the teacher walked into the room, everybody stopped talking.

Tell	
Use	**Example**
To give information to a person. Used in direct and indirect speech.	She told me that she would be late. I won't tell you to do your homework again!

Speak	
Use	**Example**
Used to refer to monologues or serious conversation or to refer to the knowledge of other languages.	I'll have to speak to that boy – he's getting very lazy. She speaks three languages fluently.

Page 16

To represent the speech of other people or what we say can be done in two different ways:

- by using the **direct speech** with quotation marks:

"I work in a bank."

- by using the **reported speech**:

He said he worked in a bank.

He said that he traveled a lot on business.

In the reported speech the tenses, word order and pronouns may be different from those in the original sentence. Look how the changes occur:

Direct speech	Indirect speech
Simple present	**Past tense**
I am in Paris!	She said that she was in Paris.
Present continuous	**Past continuous**
I am shopping a lot.	She said that she was shopping a lot.
Simple past	**Past perfect**
I drove a Ferrari.	She said she had driven a Ferrari.
Past continuous	**Past perfect continuous**
I was driving a Ferrari.	She said that she had been driving a Ferrari.
Present perfect	**Past perfect**
I have driven a Ferrari.	She said that she had driven a Ferrari.
Will	**Would**
I will drive a Ferrari.	She said she would drive a Ferrari.
Must	**Had to**
I must drive a Ferrari.	She said that she had to drive a Ferrari.
Can	**Could**
I can drive a Ferrari.	She said that she could drive a Ferrari.
May	**Might**
I may drive a Ferrari.	She said that she might drive a Ferrari.
Could, should, might	**Could, should, might**
I could drive a Ferrari.	She said that she could drive a Ferrari.

Page 18

To connect two events or actions at a point of time in the speech we use time expressions like **when**, **before** and **after**. Look at their uses:

When	Place one of the events / actions at a specific time conditioned to other event / action.	1st clause	2nd clause
		Present	**Present**
		Tom makes dinner **when** he gets home every night.	
		Present	**Future**
		When Tom gets his points, he will exchange them for candy.	
		Past	**Past**
		Tom made dinner **when** he got home last night.	
Before	Place one of the events / actions at an earlier time than the other events / actions.	**Present**	**Present**
		Tom takes a shower **before** he has breakfast.	
		Present	**Future**
		Before Tom calls the dentist, he will take a shower.	
		Past	**Past**
		Before Tom called the dentist, he took a shower.	
After	Place one of the events / actions at a later time than the other events / actions.	**Present**	**Present**
		Tom takes a shower **after** he cleans the house.	
		Present	**Future**
		After Tom cleans the house, he will have some relaxing time.	
		Past	**Past**
		Tom took a shower **after** he cleaned the house yesterday.	

||| Unit 2 |||

Page 29

If two things are equal in some way, it can be expressed by using the **comparison of equality** involving the adjectives. The structure is:

- "**as** _adjective_ **as**"

Mr. Murdoch's bull is **as** _heavy_ **as** a small elephant.

- "_not_ **as** _adjective_ **as**".

Mr. Murdoch's bull is _not_ **as** _heavy_ **as** a small elephant.

Page 30

If two things are different in some way, it can be expressed by using the **comparative** form of the adjectives. The structure is "**comparative adjective** _than_", and there are two different forms depending on the number of syllables of the adjective:

- To one-syllable or some two-syllable adjectives, it is added the suffix (**-er**):

A bear is **small_er_ _than_** an elephant.

– If the adjective ends with a consonant, it doubles the consonant and add the suffix:

Jane is **bigg_er_ _than_** her cousin.

– If the adjective ends with a consonant followed by the semivowel (**-y**), the semivowel is eliminated and the suffix (**-ier**) is added:

Carlos is **bus_ier_ _than_** Thomas is.

- To two/three or more syllable adjectives, it is added the word **_more_** before the adjective:

Carrie is _more_ **excited** with the school recital _than Carol_.

Page 31

The comparison of more than two things that are different in some way can be expressed by using the **superlative** form of the adjectives. There are two different forms depending on the number of syllables of the adjective:

- To one-syllable or some two-syllable adjectives, it is added the word _the_ before the adjective and the suffix (**-est**):

Fleas are _the_ **small_est_** insects that I know.

– If the adjective ends with a consonant, it doubles the consonant and add the suffix:

Jane is _the_ **biggest** fan of Taylor Swift.

– If the adjective ends with a consonant followed by the semivowel (**-y**), the semivowel is eliminated and the suffix (**-iest**) is added:

Carlos is _the_ **bus_iest_** man I know.

- To two/three or more syllable adjectives, it is added the words _the most_ before the adjective:

Carrie is _the most_ **excited** about the school recital.

||| Unit 3 |||

Page 47 to 49

We use the **present perfect** to say that an action happened at an **unspecified** time before now. We use it when we talk about an action or state which started in the past and continues up to the present time. For example:

Get to know food you**'ve** never **tasted** before!

Find out about different places you **haven't visited** yet!

Observe that this tense always uses an auxiliary verb (**have/has**) and the **past participle of the verb**. When we talk about **regular verbs**, the past participle has the same form as the **simple past**. Look at the sentence structure of the present perfect tense:

- Affirmative

Subject pronoun + **auxiliary verb** + **verb in the past participle** + complement

Susan has washed her car.

Timmy and Tammy have traveled to Canada.

- Negative

Subject pronoun + **auxiliary verb** + **not** + **verb in the past participle** + complement

Susan has not (**hasn't**) **washed** her car.

Timmy and Tammy have not (**haven't**) **traveled** to Canada.

- Interrogative

Auxiliary verb + **subject pronoun** + **verb in the past participle** + complement

Has Susan washed her car?

Have Timmy and Tammy traveled to Canada?

||| Unit 4 |||

Page 59 to 62

The past participle form of irregular verbs are all different and learning them just takes practice. There is a list of irregular verbs to learn from and you can look it up at the end of the book.

There are two ways to measure time in the present perfect tense. Either we use **for** or **since**.

- **For** is used when we measure how long something lasts and it always indicates a period of time, like years, weeks, months, hours etc.

Susan hasn't washed her car **for** three weeks now.

- **Since** is used to indicate when something has started, it refers to when something began. It always indicates a specific point in time, like this morning, last month, 5 o'clock etc.

Susan hasn't washed her car **since** January 3rd.

When the present perfect tense is used to enquire people about experiences the adverb **ever** is used, which means "at any time". This adverb is always used in questions, to indicate first experiences or used with *nothing* and *nobody* for things that haven't happened before. The **adverb** is placed between the auxiliary and the main verb.

Have you **ever** played golf?

Nobody has **ever** traveled through time.

This is the first time I've **ever** eaten snake soup.

When the present perfect tense is used to **express something that has not happened at all**, the adverb **never** is used. The **adverb** is placed between the auxiliary and the main verb.

I've **never** lived abroad.

She has **never** driven a car.

There are some adverbs that are often used with the present perfect tense to identify or express a time for the happening. These adverbs are:

- **Just** means '*a short time ago*'. It comes between the auxiliary and the main verb.

Mike has just called.

Mom and dad have just arrived.

- **Already** means something has happened early – or earlier than it should have. It is used in affirmative sentences and comes between the auxiliary and the main verb.
I've **already** watched all the episodes of my favorite series.
The bus has **already** left. I'm going to be late for school.
- **Yet** means something is expected to happen. It means '*at any time up to now*'. It is used in questions and negatives and it usually comes at the end of the sentence.
Have you finished your homework **yet**?
I haven't finished my homework **yet**.

||| Unit 5 |||

Page 77

The terms **A.D.** (*Anno Domini*) and **b.C.** (*before Christ*) are used to label or number years in the Gregorian calendar. This calendar is the most world widely used and it is based on the traditionally reckoned year of Jesus Christ birth, which is considered the year one. Therefore, **A.D.** counts years from the start of this era, and **b.C.** the years before it.

Page 78

Take a look at how **big numbers** are written in full.

	Explanation	Example
Hundred	Indicates a cardinal number between 100 and 999. It is indicated by telling: number + hundred.	100 – one hundred 210 – two hundred ten 869 – eight hundred sixty-nine 943 – nine hundred forty-three
Thousand	Indicates a cardinal number between 1,000 and 9,999. It is indicated by telling: number + thousand.	1,000 – one thousand 2,110 – two thousand one hundred ten 8,669 – eight thousand six hundred sixty-nine 9,443 – nine thousand four hundred forty-three
Million	Indicates a cardinal number between 1,000,000 and 1,999,999. It is indicated by telling: number + million.	1,000,000 – one million 2,200,110 – two million two hundred thousand one hundred ten 8,080,669 – eight million eighty thousand six hundred sixty-nine 9,009,443 – nine million nine thousand four hundred forty-three

Page 79 and 80

The **simple past tense** refers to actions, events and happenings that are finished and have no connection with the present time. Usually, it indicates **when** something happened.
You took a trip **last year**.
She visited some art galleries **in 2011**.

The adverb **ago** is used with the **simple past tense** to indicate how much time has passed since the action/event happened.

We <u>drove</u> across Europe **five months ago**.

I <u>got married</u> ten years **ago**.

I <u>bought</u> it six months **ago**.

The **present perfect tense** refers to actions, events, and happenings that are not yet finished. It began in some point in the past, but it still has some connection or result in the present time.

You <u>have taken</u> a trip **this year**.

We <u>have driven</u> across Europe **many times**.

The preposition **for** is used with the **present perfect tense** to indicate the duration of the action/event up to the present moment.

She has been in Ireland **for** three days.

You have been my friend **for** ten years.

||| Unit 6 |||

Check out some **adjectives** to describe **physical appearance**.

Category	Adjective		Adjective	
Height	tall		adventurous	undisturbed
	average height		angry	unfriendly
	short		bored	ungenerous
Hair length	long		boring	unhappy
	medium		calm	unhesitant
	short		cautious	unreliable
	bald	**Personality**	clumsy	unselfish
Hair color	dark hair / brunet (men) / brunette (women)		courageous	unsurprised
	brown hair		dishonest	unworried
	blond (men) / blonde (women)		disorganized	uptight
	red hair		disrespectful	worried
	gray hair		dissatisfied	
	dyed / stained hair		easygoing	

Hair style	straight	fearful	
	wavy	friendly	
	curly	fun	
	afro	generous	
Weight	fat / chubby	happy	
	average built	hardworking	
	slim / thin	helpful	
Eyes	brown	hesitant	
	black	honest	
	green	imaginative	
	blue	impatient	
	hazel	inconsiderate	
Personality	indifferent	**Personality**	respectful
	insensitive	rude	
	irresolute	satisfied	
	kind	selfish	
	lazy	sensitive	
	loyal	shocked	
	mean	skillful	
	organized	surprised	
	patient	nice	
	persistent	tense	
	polite	thrilled	
	relaxed	uncreative	
	reliable	respectful	

Other characteristics	blind	wrinkles	mustache
	hunchbacked	freckles	beard
	dark circles	pimples	wear glasses
	wart	scar	wear braces

Page 93

An adjective that ends with the suffix **-ing** is used to describe the **characteristics** of a person or a thing.

My girlfriend is **boring**. (My girlfriend is a boring person.)

I am **confusing**. (I will cause you to be confused.)

An adjective that ends with the suffix **-ed** is used to describe a **feeling** caused by someone or something.

My girlfriend is **bored**. (My girlfriend feels bored.)

I am **confused**. (I don't understand something.)

Page 95

The **relative pronouns** are used to connect sentences, and their use depends on what they refer to.

• **Who** – it is used to refer to **people**.

Aisha is a baby girl. She has cried nonstop! ⟶ Aisha is the baby girl who has cried nonstop.

• **Which** – it is used to refer to **animals** or **things**.

They said a date. The date is my birthday. ⟶ They said a date **which** is my birthday.

• **Whose** – it is used to indicate possession by people and animals, or even things (in formal situations).

Bob has a daughter. The name of Bob's daughter is Leanne. ⟶ Bob has a daughter **whose** name is Leanne.

||| Unit 7 |||

Page 111

The form of the verb that ends with the suffix **-ing** is called a **gerund** when used as a <u>noun</u>. There are some verbs that must be followed by a gerund. Examples:

My father really **enjoys cooking**.

Do you **mind helping** me with my homework?

You shouldn't **give up doing** things that make you happy.

Daisy **recommended trying** Poutine in Canada.

The following verbs **must** be followed by a gerund.

• admit	• give up	• put off
• avoid	• go + activities	• quit
• consider	• keep on	• recommend
• discuss	• mind	• resist
• dislike	• miss	• stop (= quit)
• enjoy	• postpone	• suggest
• finish	• practice	• think about

Verbs that show emotion and the fulfillment or unfulfillment of an activity may affect the meaning depending on the choice of an infinitive or a gerund. Gerunds are used to describe actions that are factual, whereas infinitives are used to describe actions that may take place in the time to come or that are possible. Verbs like *hear, notice, observe, see, watch* may be followed by both gerunds or infinitive. The infinitive without *to* often emphasizes the whole action or event which someone hears or sees. The (*-ing*) – *gerund* – form usually emphasizes an action or event which is in progress or not yet completed. Examples:

She **saw** her son **swim** in the competition. – The whole event was observed.

I **heard** my father **arriving** at home. – The action was in progress, not completed.

The following verbs are followed by infinitives.

- agree
- appear
- expect
- forget
- hope
- learn
- mean

- need
- offer
- seem
- try
- want
- would like

Examples:

He **decided to visit** Europe instead of the USA.

I **tried to talk** to Elliot but he didn't pick up his phone.

My sister **promised to take** me to the movies tonight.

I would **like to meet** your mother, she seems lovely.

The following verbs may be followed by either a gerund or an infinitive.

- attempt
- begin
- cannot
- continue
- dread
- hate
- intend
- like

- love
- plan
- prefer
- stand
- start
- stop
- try

||| Unit 8 |||

Page 125

The **modal verb can** is used to express knowledge of how to do something; the physical or mental ability to do something; the possibility of doing something; or even permission to do something.

- Its affirmative form is:
  Subject pronoun + **can** + **main verb in the infinitive** + complement.
  I can do the homework.
  You can play the piano.
- Its negative form is **cannot** or **can't**.
  I cannot (**can't**) **do** the homework.
  You cannot (**can't**) **play** the piano.
- Its interrogative form is:
  Can I do the homework?
  Can you play the piano?

The **modal verb should** is used to express obligation, duty or to make a suggestion about something (good) to be done.

- Its affirmative form is:
  Subject pronoun + **should** + **main verb in the infinitive** + complement.
  Tom doesn't study enough. **He should study** harder.
  It's a good film. **You should go** and see it.
- Its negative form is **shouldn't**.
  Tom shouldn't go to bed late. He wakes up really tired.
  You shouldn't eat junk food all the time. You are putting on some weight.
- Its interrogative form is:
  Should I ask Danny about his breaking up with Jenny?

Page 126

The **graded quantifiers** are used to talk about the quantity of something. They vary according to the nouns they accompany, it means, they can be **countable** or **uncountable**.

Quantifiers used with countable nouns	
many	There are **many** people living in Africa.
(a) few	I bought **few** fruits in the supermarket.
fewer (than)	**Fewer** students came to school yesterday.
Quantifiers used with uncountable nouns	
much	There wasn't **much** snow in the garden.
(a) little	There was **little** information about that city.
less (than)	Janet had **less** time to study than Sophie.
Quantifiers used with both, countable and uncountable nouns	
enough	They have **enough** money to buy lunch.
more	Paul needs to eat **more** vegetables.

IRREGULAR VERBS

BASE FORM OF VERB	SIMPLE PAST	PAST PARTICIPLE
be	was / were	been
beat	beat	beaten
become	became	become
begin	began	begun
bet	bet	bet
blow	blew	blown
break	broke	broken
bring	brought	brought
build	built	built
burst	burst	burst
buy	bought	bought
catch	caught	caught
choose	chose	chosen
come	came	come
cost	cost	cost
cut	cut	cut
deal	dealt	dealt
do	did	done
draw	drew	drawn
drink	drank	drunk
drive	drove	driven
eat	ate	eaten
fall	fell	fallen
feed	fed	fed
feel	felt	felt
fight	fought	fought
find	found	found
fly	flew	flown
forget	forgot	forgotten
freeze	froze	frozen
get	got	got / gotten
give	gave	given
go	went	gone

IRREGULAR VERBS

BASE FORM OF VERB	SIMPLE PAST	PAST PARTICIPLE
grow	grew	grown
hang	hung	hung
have	had	had
hear	heard	heard
hide	hid	hidden
hit	hit	hit
hold	held	held
hurt	hurt	hurt
keep	kept	kept
know	knew	known
lay	laid	laid
lead	led	led
leave	left	left
lend	lent	lent
let	let	let
lie	lay	lain
light	lit	lit
lose	lost	lost
make	made	made
mean	meant	meant
meet	met	met
pay	paid	paid
put	put	put
read	read	read
ride	rode	ridden
ring	rang	rung
rise	rose	risen
run	ran	run
say	said	said
see	saw	seen
sell	sold	sold
send	sent	sent
set	set	set

BASE FORM OF VERB	SIMPLE PAST	PAST PARTICIPLE
shake	shook	shaken
shine	shone	shone
shoot	shot	shot
show	showed	shown
shut	shut	shut
sing	sang	sung
sink	sank	sunk
sit	sat	sat
sleep	slept	slept
slide	slid	slid
speak	spoke	spoken
spend	spent	spent
spring	sprang	sprung
stand	stood	stood
steal	stole	stolen
stick	stuck	stuck
swear	swore	sworn
sweep	swept	swept
swim	swam	swum
swing	swung	swung
take	took	taken
teach	taught	taught
tear	tore	torn
tell	told	told
think	thought	thought
throw	threw	thrown
understand	understood	understood
wake	woke	woken
wear	wore	worn
weave	wove	woven
win	won	won
write	wrote	written

GLOSSARY

A

a good ol' (a good and old): um bom e velho

a step at a time: um passo por vez

ablaze: em chamas

able-bodied: sem deficiência física

Aboriginal: aborígine

abstain: abster-se

achieve: alcançar

acquaintance: conhecido

across: através de

actor: ator

actress: atriz

Adaptive Sport: esporte adaptado

address: endereço

after: depois

aim: objetivo

allowance: mesada

alongside: junto com

amazing: maravilhoso; surpreendente

amount: quantidade

ancient: antigo

angry: bravo

appreciation: apreciação

April Fool's Day: Dia da mentira; primeiro de abril

April: abril

archery: tiro com arco

arrive: chegar

aspire: ambicionar

athletics: atletismo

attend: participar

attentively: atentamente

avoid: evitar

award: prêmio

B

back "clap": batida nas costas

bad: ruim; mau

bag: mala; bagagem

bake: assar

based: sediado

be held: ser realizado

beans: feijões

beautiful: bonito

become: tornar-se

bed: cama

bedroom: quarto

before: antes

benefit: beneficiar-se, vantagem

best-known: mais conhecido

bet: apostar

better: melhor

bill: conta

birthday: aniversário

bit: um pouco

blind: cego

blindness: cegueira

booking: reserva

boring: chato

bow: reverência

Brazilian: brasileiro(a)

breakfast: café da manhã

bridge: ponte

brother: irmão

brush: escovar

build on: construir

bump into: esbarrar

bursting at the seams (slang): lugar que abriga um grande número de pessoas ou coisas; excessivamente lotado (gíria)

C

cake: bolo

call on: recorrer; apelar

canoeing: canoagem

Carnival: carnaval

carol singing: cânticos de Natal

carrot: cenoura

carve: esculpir

carving: entalhe; escultura

celebrate: comemorar

celebration: celebração

ceremony: cerimônia

change: mudança

chatty: que gosta de conversar (tagarela)

cheerful: alegre

cheetah: guepardo

chef: chefe de cozinha

Chinese New Year: Ano Novo Chinês

Chinese: chinês; chinesa

Christmas: Natal

citizen: cidadão; cidadã

closure: fechamento

clumsy: desajeitado

cold cuts: frios (carnes pré-cozidas ou defumadas, como presunto, salame etc.)

cold weather: tempo frio; inverno

cold: frio

combine: combinar; misturar

come down: encontrar-se com alguém em algum lugar

comeback: retorno

commemorative date: data comemorativa

commonly: comumente

commonwealth: comunidade política

composer: compositor
composting: compostagem
continue on: continuar
cook: cozinhar
cooperative: colaborativo
costume: traje; fantasia
country: país
crowded: cheio de gente
customs: alfândega
cycling: ciclismo

D

dairy: laticínio
dark blue: azul-escuro
Day of the Dead: Dia dos Mortos; Dia de Finados
deal: lidar
death: morte
December: dezembro
deep down: no fundo
deep: profundo; fundo
deliver: entregar
depict: retratar
develop: desenvolver
dietary: alimentar
dinner: jantar
disability: deficiência
dishonest: desonesto
display: exibição
distressed: angustiado
dock: doca
dozen: dúzia
drink: beber
driver: motorista
dye: corante; tinta
dystrophy: distrofia

E

eager: ansioso
early: no começo
earn: ganhar
easter egg: ovo de páscoa

Easter: Páscoa
eat: comer
embarrassed: envergonhado
embassy: embaixada
engineer: engenheiro
engraving: gravura
enrich: enriquecer
ensuing: resultante
enthusiastic: entusiasmado
envious: invejoso
envision: imaginar
ethics: ética
exchange: trocar

F

faithful: fiel
family: família
faster (fast): mais rápido
father: pai
Father's Day: Dia dos Pais
feast: banquete; celebração
feature: característica
feeling: sentimento
feline: felino
fencing: esgrima
ferry: balsa
fewer: menos
field mission: missão de campo
figure: aparência
find out: descobrir
first: primeiro
food: comida
food-scrap: lixo orgânico
football: futebol americano; (UK): futebol
forehead: testa
France: França
friend: amigo
frog: sapo

full-size: tamanho completo; real
funny/fun: engraçado; divertido

G

gallery: galeria
game: jogo
gathering: reunião; encontro
get involved: participar; envolver-se
gift: presente
glaucoma: glaucoma (doença causada pela elevação da pressão intraocular, pode levar à cegueira quando não tratada)
goal: meta
gold: ouro
good tempered: equilibrado
good: bom; boa
Goodwill Ambassador: embaixador da boa vontade
gorgeous: lindo
gradually: gradualmente
Greece: Grécia
greet: cumprimentar
grocery: mercearia
gruesomely: de forma horrível, repulsiva
guidebook: guia
gymnastics: ginástica

H

hair: cabelo
Halloween: Dia das Bruxas
handshake: aperto de mão
hang out: sair com alguém
Hanukkah: Chanucá; Hanucá; Festival das luzes
happy: feliz
hardworking: trabalhador; esforçado

head swivel: giro de cabeça
head to: se direcionar; dirigir para
health: saúde
hear: ouvir
heritage: herança
hold: manter
holiday: feriado
hollow out: escavar
home/house: casa
homework: lição de casa
honor: honrar
hope: esperança
horrible: horrível
host (noun): anfitrião; anfitriã
host (verb): hospedar; abrigar
humble: humilde
hundred: cem

I

ice cream: sorvete
ice sledge: trenó de gelo
illness: doença
immerse: mergulhar; imergir
increase: aumentar
incredible: inacreditável
indigenous: indígena
injured: ferido
issue: emitir
Italy: Itália

J

January: janeiro
Japanese: japonês; japonesa
judge: juiz
jump: pular
June: junho
jungle: selva

K

keep in mind: ter em mente

keep up with: acompanhar; estar a par de
kid: criança

L

largest: maior
lawyer: advogado
lazy: preguiçoso
left out (feel left out): sentir-se excluído
legendary: lendário
library: biblioteca
light pink: rosa-claro
light up: acender; iluminar
lighthouse: farol
limb: membro do corpo; parte
live up to: agir de acordo com
locals: residentes locais
long before: muito antes
long face (slang): triste; desapontado (gíria)
long-time: há muito tempo; antigo
look after: cuidar de
look around: olhar ao redor
look up: procurar
lose one's sight: perder a visão
lower: reduzir

M

mainland: continente
major: principal
make: fazer
March: março
match: igualar; combinar
meal: refeição
mean: maldoso
meat: carne
merely: apenas
messy: desorganizado
midnight: meia-noite
might: poderia

milk: leite
million: milhão
miss out: perder
mistake: erro
mobility: mobilidade
money: dinheiro
monsoon: monção
month: mês
mood: humor
morning: manhã
Mother's Day: Dia das Mães
motherhood: maternidade
muddy yourself up: enlamear-se
musician: músico

N

nap: cochilo; soneca
neighbor: vizinho
Netherlands: Países Baixos (Holanda)
New Year's Day: Dia de Ano Novo
nonprofits: sem fins lucrativos
nose: nariz
nothing: nada
nurse: enfermeiro
nut: noz

O

October: outubro
oldest: mais antigo
once-in-a-lifetime: uma vez na vida
orange: laranja
outgoing: extrovertido
overall: no geral
overnight: da noite para o dia

P

paint: pintar
painting: pintura

palsy: paralisia
parade: parada
party: festa
pass: falecer
path: caminho; vereda
patron: patrono
people: pessoas
perhaps: possivelmente
pictures: fotografias
pie: torta
place: lugar
plan out: planejar
play: jogar
player: jogador
pleasant: agradável
plethora: abundância
policeman: policial
polite: educado
port city: cidade portuária
poultry: carne de aves
precede: preceder
prescription: receita médica
prom: baile de formatura
prosthesis: prótese
proud: orgulhoso
purely: puramente
purple: roxo
purpose: propósito
pursue: buscar; ir atrás de algo
push: dar uma forçada; forçar
put aside: pôr de lado

Q

R

rain-showers: pancadas de chuva
raise: levantar; aumentar; elevar; provocar; motivar
random: aleatório
receive: receber
reciprocity: reciprocidade

recognise: reconhecer
recognition: reconhecimento
red ochre: ocre vermelho
red: vermelho
refined: refinado; processado
refrain: evitar
refugee camp: campo de refugiados
relaxed: relaxado
religious: religioso
report: relatar
rest: descansar
resurrection: ressurreição
retail: varejo
rich: rico
rinse off: enxaguar
rock climbing: escalada
rock shelter: abrigo rochoso
role model: modelo
rowing: remo
run into: topar com
run: durar; ter validade
running: corrida
Russian: russo, russa

S

sacred site: local sagrado
sad: triste
Saint Patrick's Day: Dia de São Patrício
saint: santo
salesclerk: balconista
satisfied: satisfeito
Saturday: sábado
school: escola
scientist: cientista
score: pontuar
scouted: termo usado em esportes para observar talentos promissores
scuba diving: mergulho autônomo
seed: semente

seemingly: aparentemente
self-esteem: autoestima
selfish: egoísta
self-worth: autoestima
serving: porção
settle: decidir-se
share: compartilhar
shocked: chocado
shortly: (em) pouco tempo
shower: chuveiro; banho
shush: silenciar
shy: tímido
sick: doente
singer: cantor
ski: esquiar
skiing: esqui
skill: habilidade
skilled: especializado
skydiving: paraquedismo
sleep: dormir
slice: fatia
smooch: beijo
snake: cobra
snow: neve
snowball fight: guerra de bolas de neve
snowmen: bonecos de neve
soccer: futebol
soil: solo
songwriter: letrista
Spain: Espanha
Spanish: espanhol, espanhola
sparingly: com moderação
special: especial
spider: aranha
spill: derramar
spinal cord injuries: lesões da medula espinhal
spoken: falado
sport: esporte
stand out: destacar-se
stay on (one's) toes: ficar atento
step up: reforçar

stinks (slang): é muito ruim; uma porcaria (gíria)
story: história
street: rua
stuck: preso
student: estudante
such as: tal como
sugary: açucarado
sunflower: girassol
supply: fornecer
support: suporte; apoio
surprised: surpreso
surrounding: arredor
sustain: sustentar
swath: carreira
sweet: doce
swim: nadar

T

table tennis: tênis de mesa
take a stand: posicionar-se
take a toll on: expressão idiomática que remete a algo que causa sofrimento
take it all in: assimilar
take place: acontecer
talk: falar
tangible: tangível
tattoo: tatuar
teacher: professor
team: time
teenager: adolescente
teeth: dentes
termite: térmita (cupim)
terrain: terreno
Thailand: Tailândia
thing: coisa
thousand: mil

thrilled: emocionado
thrive: prosperar
throughout: ao longo
throw: jogar; lançar
tidy: organizado; arrumado
tied: amarrado
tired: cansado
today: hoje
tomb: tumba
tomorrow: amanhã
tourist guide: guia turístico
towering: elevando-se; imponente; muito alto
trace back: remeter
track and field: atletismo
trader: comerciante
traditional: tradicional
travel abroad: viajar para o exterior
travel: viajar
treat: agradar; cuidar; tratar
trick-or-treating: gostosuras ou travessuras
try on: experimentar

U

U-20 squad: time sub-20
United Kingdom: Reino Unido
unlike: ao contrário
untapped: inexplorado
up to date: atualizado
upset: chateado

V

vacancy: vaga
vacation: férias
visa: visto
volunteer: voluntário

W

wall: parede
warm: quente; calor
watch: assistir
water: água
week: semana
weekend: final de semana
wellbeing: bem-estar
well-choreographed slap: tapa ensaiado
well known: bem conhecido
western: ocidental
wheat: trigo
wheelchair: cadeira de rodas
whenever: sempre que; a qualquer momento
whether: se
while: enquanto
whole: todo; inteiro; completo; integral
wholesome: saudável
widely: amplamente
wonder: pensar; imaginar
wonders: maravilhas
work: trabalho
worm: verme
worried: preocupado
worst: pior
writer: escritor; autor

X

Y

yesterday: ontem
young: jovem

Z